SEP/OCT
2013

The Heart of Worship

**'Glorify the LORD with me,
let us exalt his name together.'**
Psalm 34:3

Selwyn Hughes & Philip Greenslade
Revised and updated by Mick Brooks
FURTHER STUDY: IAN SEWTER

CWR, Waverley Abbey House, Waverley Lane, Farnham, Surrey GU9 8EP, UK
Tel: 01252 784700 Email: mail@cwr.org.uk
Registered Charity No. 294387. Registered Limited Company No. 1990308.

Cover image: CWR
Quiet Time image: Fotosearch
Printed in England by Linney Print

CWR

MIX
Paper from responsible sources
FSC® C015900
FSC www.fsc.org

very Day with Jesus is available in **large print** from CWR. It is also available on **audio and DAISY**
n the UK and Eire for the sole use of those with a visual impairment worse than N12, or who are
egistered blind. For details please contact **Torch Trust for the Blind**, Tel: 01858 438260.
orch Trust for the Blind, Torch House, Torch Way, Northampton Road, Market Harborough LE16 9HL.

A word of introduction ...

It can be an amazing, spine-tingling experience to watch men sing with gusto, tears, and passion, hands raised to heaven in whole-hearted adoration; only to realise that it's just a football game!

Deep within every heart is a desire to worship: it is integral to our God-given design. The problem is that when we don't worship God we worship something else. In Selwyn's book *The 7 Laws of Spiritual Success* he makes clear that the primary purpose of mankind's creation was that we might freely and intelligently worship the Creator. But as one commentator observed, 'Whilst the contemporary church is strong in evangelism, teaching, and is making great strides in areas of social need, pastoral care, counselling and relational issues, our depth of understanding and practice of worship is sadly lacking.'

The Westminster Shorter Catechism asks the question: 'What is the chief end of man?' and answers: 'The chief end of man is to glorify God and enjoy Him for ever.'

We need to rediscover our roots and first foundations. Many personality problems arise as a result of our failure to truly worship God: C.S. Lewis believed that it is in the process of worship that God communicates His presence to us. As we worship, we open a door in our hearts to God. He comes through and gives Himself to us, so we are the beneficiaries of worship, not Him.

In this issue Selwyn explores many facets of this vital aspect of the Christian life and provides us with plenty of suggestions to truly live out a life of worship.

Sincerely yours in His name,

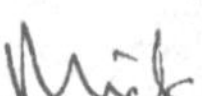

Mick Brooks, Consulting Editor

Free small group resources to accompany this issue can be found at www.cwr.org.uk/extra. The *EDWJ* Facebook community is growing! To join the conversation visit www.facebook.com/edwjpage

The Heart of Worship

SUN
1 SEP

FOR READING & MEDITATION – REVELATION 5:1–14

'Worthy is the Lamb, who was slain, to receive ... honour and glory and praise!' (v.12)

No greater theme could ever occupy our attention than the one we are about to consider: the worship of God. A.W. Tozer, writing in the middle of the last century, said, 'Worship is the missing jewel of the evangelical church'. In some ways not much has changed since Tozer wrote those striking words for over the past decades the Holy Spirit has been renewing His Church in a wonderful way and bringing Christians of all denominations to a new understanding of the meaning of worship. However, there is still much to learn if we are to explore the depths of this vitally important subject.

In today's passage the apostle John catches a brief glimpse of the worship being offered in heaven – the kind of worship that is to be offered on earth. When we cry from the depth of our beings and with the utmost sincerity 'Worthy is the Lamb' then we come near to the heart of worship. 'Worship' is simply to ascribe 'worth' to what we value the most, and no one is more worthy of our reverence and praise than the one Creator God Himself. The more we contemplate the majesty of God the more we are drawn to Him. When we are moved by a magnificent sunset or by a field of beautiful flowers our natural response is to gasp, 'Oh, how beautiful'. How much greater, then, could be our response when we consider who God is and what He does.

In his letter to the Romans, Paul pours out his feelings after reflecting on the riches of God's grace. For a moment he pauses in worship and then he exclaims, 'Oh, the depth of the riches of the wisdom and knowledge of God' (Rom. 11:33)! Amazement and wonder are always the natural response to the contemplation of God's mercy and grace.

FURTHER STUDY

John 1:29; Rev. 4:1–11

1. Why is the Lamb worthy of worship?

2. Why is God worthy of worship?

Gracious Father, as I begin this adventure of discovery and learn what it means to worship You in spirit and in truth I ask that You will help me to gain a deeper understanding of this issue than I have ever had before. In Jesus' name. Amen.

Offering our whole selves

FOR READING & MEDITATION – ROMANS 12:1–8

'... I urge you ... in view of God's mercy, to offer your bodies as living sacrifices, holy and pleasing to God ...' (v.1)

It may be argued that there is a subtle difference between worship and praise. Some say we *praise* God for what He does and we *worship* Him for who He is. In these meditations, however, the term 'worship' is being used in its broadest sense to describe our heartfelt response to God and His goodness. That response may be praise, thanksgiving, blessing, service, or even, as we shall see, lament.

In today's reading Paul describes worship as the offering of our whole selves as a living sacrifice to God. Worship involves our response to God not only when we go to church on a Sunday but also in what we do from Monday to Saturday. What happens when worshippers gather together on a Sunday is conceived to be the concentration, the summing-up and focus of what all life is about. Frequently there is a tendency in many churches to regard praise and worship as something that is done at the beginning of a service, led by a 'worship leader', rather than to see the whole service as being an act of worship. It is just as much worship to give in the offering as it is to sing, 'O worship the King, all glorious above'. In church on a Sunday the individual worship given to God from Monday to Saturday is brought together in a corporate act. That is one of the prime purposes of the Church – to worship God *collectively*.

FURTHER STUDY

Psa. 35:9–10; Mark 12:28–31; Eph. 6:5–9

1. How did the psalmist worship?

2. How should we worship God?

Worship relates not only to the songs we sing, the prayers we pray, and the thanks we give, but to everything we do when we gather together as the people of God. A leader who says, 'Let's have a time of worship before we listen to the message,' shows that he or she doesn't fully understand what true worship involves. Worship does not stop when the sermon starts.

Gracious Father, help me not to compartmentalise life but to see it as a whole. May I accept that worship is what You expect from me not one day of the week but every day of the week. In Jesus' name. Amen.

How do you see God?

TUES
3 SEP

FOR READING & MEDITATION – ROMANS 1:18–25

'For although they knew God, they neither glorified him as God nor gave thanks to him ...' (v.21)

In today's reading the apostle Paul suggests that one aspect of sin is a failure to worship the Creator. Our instinct to worship is God-given. We were created to worship. It is possible to observe a faint echo of this design in our instinctive need to applaud great performers or in our adulation of celebrities and other music and sports personalities. Sin, however, perverts this innate desire to worship God and diverts it to lesser objects. 'They neither glorified him as God nor gave thanks to him ... and worshipped and served created things rather than the Creator' (Rom. 1:21,25). The late Francis Schaeffer said, 'The beginning of man's rebellion against God was, and is, the lack of a thankful heart ... The rebellion is the deliberate refusal to be the creature before the Creator, to the extent of being thankful.'

Paul talks also in this passage about those who '... exchanged the glory of the immortal God for images made to look like mortal man and birds and animals and reptiles' (v.23). There is another name for this – *idolatry*. Idolatry, however, is not only the worship of false gods; it can also be the worship of the true God in a false way. In the words of A.W. Tozer, 'Idolatry is the entertaining of ideas about God that are unworthy of Him.'

How do you see God? What concept of the Father do you carry deep down in your heart? What thoughts form in your mind and what feelings are aroused within you when you see that short yet profound three-lettered word: *God*? The answers to those questions will determine the depth or superficiality of your worship. We do not truly worship God if we carry in our hearts a wrong or unworthy concept of Him. That is a law that is as fixed as the law of gravity.

FURTHER STUDY

Psa. 86:5–15; Matt. 25:24–25

1. How did the psalmist see God?

2. How did the wicked servant see the good master?

O Father, if this is true then I need to do some serious thinking. Teach me the truth about Yourself so that the picture I carry in my mind is one that accords with Scripture. In Jesus' name I pray. Amen.

Christian idolaters

FOR READING & MEDITATION – EPHESIANS 1:3–14

'Praise be to the God and Father of our Lord Jesus Christ, who has blessed us ... with every spiritual blessing in Christ.' (v.3)

The whole subject of worship rises and falls according to our understanding and concept of God. We simply do not worship God in the way He created us to worship until we understand something of who He is. What comes into our minds when we think about God is most important. Worship is pure or base according to whether the worshipper considers high or low thoughts about God. A wrong concept of Him will lead to wrong conclusions about Him. For example, if you entertain the thought that God does not have your highest interests at heart then it will most certainly affect the way you worship Him. You cannot worship someone you don't trust.

Each one of us would do well to pause and ask again the questions we posed yesterday: What is my image of God? How do I see Him? What concept of the Creator do I carry in my heart? How, for instance, does the picture the apostle Paul gives of God in the verses before us today compare with your own image of God? Is it similar or radically different? The reason why Paul could speak of God so powerfully was because He saw Him clearly.

Following on from what we said yesterday about idolatry, it is worth noting this statement made by Dr E. Stanley Jones: 'The Church is filled with Christian idolaters, for idolatry consists not only in kneeling before visible objects and giving them obeisance but also of carrying in our hearts a picture of God which is unworthy of Him'. The idolatrous heart assumes that God is other than He is and substitutes for the true God one made after its own likeness. We need to ensure our concept of God is drawn from Scripture, otherwise we may be holding in our minds a false picture of Him.

FURTHER STUDY

John 16:1–4; Acts 17:22–31

1. Why would Christians suffer persecutions?

2. What well-meaning error did Paul expose?

My Father and my God, I realise I am dealing here with a key issue. Help me draw my understanding of You not from what others say about You but from what You say about Yourself. In Jesus' name. Amen.

'Your God is my devil'

FOR READING & MEDITATION – HEBREWS 11:1–16

'... anyone who comes to [God] must believe that he exists and that he rewards those who earnestly seek him.' (v.6)

We continue considering the fact that wrong understanding about God affects the way we worship Him. On one occasion Martin Luther said to some of his critics, 'Your God is my devil'. That's rather a strange comment to make, you might think, but Luther was taking to task the priests of his day who thought of and portrayed God as predominantly stern, punitive, demanding and angry. They seemed to know nothing of the love that God had for His children in sending His Son to be their Saviour. In other words, they carried a concept of God that was unworthy of Him. Luther himself viewed God in those harsh terms early in his life. However, one day as he received a revelation from Scripture it revolutionised his concept of God, and that revelation led to what we now call the Reformation.

If you could be present in a Christian counselling room when a counsellee is asked 'How do you see God?' you would be astonished at some of the answers that are given. This is how one woman answered that question: 'I see God as cold, distant, unconcerned and uncommunicative, always angry with me, pushing me to do this and that for Him, but never coming through for me when I need an urgent answer to prayer.' Would it surprise you to learn that that woman struggled to worship? How can you give yourself to a God in whom you have no confidence? One challenge, therefore, of the counsellor was to help that woman reconsider her image of God.

We need to be careful that we do not entertain in our minds any unworthy thoughts about God – thoughts that misinterpret Him. The text before us today tells us the truth about God: He does reward those who earnestly seek Him.

FURTHER STUDY

Deut. 12:28–32; Matt. 15:1–9

1. How did the Canaanites' false thoughts lead to false worship?

2. Why may our worship be in vain?

Father, day by day I am realising how vital it is to have a right concept of You to worship You. I bring my whole being to You to be changed and challenged. I long to see You as You really are. Please help me, Father. In Jesus' name. Amen.

Trust – the basis of worship

FOR READING & MEDITATION – GENESIS 22:1–19

'... "Stay here with the donkey ... We will worship and then we will come back to you."' (v.5)

Having laid down a foundation for our meditations on the theme of worship, we begin now a journey through the Scriptures, starting with the Old Testament, to observe what various writers have to say about this subject.

The very first mention of the word 'worship' in the Bible occurs in the passage before us today. Abraham, at God's command, is about to set out to sacrifice his son on an altar on one of the mountains in the region of Moriah. Before he begins the ascent he instructs his servants to stay with the donkey while he and Isaac go up the mountain to erect an altar and offer a sacrifice to God. Notice again his words to the servants: 'We will worship and then we will come back to you'. These words lead us to believe that when Abraham said, '... we will come back to you,' he fully expected that despite God's earlier command to offer his son Isaac as a sacrifice he would return together with the boy.

What an astonishing faith Abraham had in God. If at this point you had been able to ask Abraham the question 'How do you see God?' what do you think he would have said? Probably something along these lines: 'God is faithful to His promises. He will not go back on His word. He has promised me that my descendants will number a great multitude so if Isaac is to die then I have no doubt God will raise him from the dead. I trust the Almighty no matter what' (see Heb. 11:17–19).

Notice also that Abraham's desire to worship God was not in any way diminished by the fact that God had told him to sacrifice his only son. And why? Because in a heart in which there is a confident trust in God there will always be a readiness to worship – even in the face of massive confusion.

FURTHER STUDY

2 Sam. 12:16–23; Dan. 3:13–30

1. How did David worship in the face of confusion?

2. How did the three Hebrews combine trust and confusion?

O Father, help me to develop a confident trust in You for I see clearly that where there is no trust there can be no true worship. In Jesus' name I pray. Amen.

CWR Ministry Events

PLEASE PRAY FOR THE TEAM

DATE	EVENT	PLACE	PRESENTER(S)
5 Sep	Insight into Bereavement	Pilgrim Hall	Peter Jackson
7 Sep	Living Singly for God's Glory	Waverley Abbey House	Julia Morgan
12 Sep	Discovering Your Spiritual Gifts	WAH	Andy Peck
13 Sep	MBTI® Personality, Prayer and Spirituality	WAH	Lynn Penson
16–20 Sep	September Country Break	PH	Ewart Helyar
21 Sep	Vital Tools for a Small Group Leader	WAH	Andy Peck
23–25 Sep	Letter to the Hebrews	WAH	Philip Greenslade
26 Sep	Career Changes and Choices	WAH	Ros and Stephen Derges
28 Sep	Christians at Work	WAH	Beverley Shepherd
11–13 Oct	Marriage on Track	WAH	Lynn and Andrew Penson
11 Oct	Bible in a Day	WAH	Andy Peck
14–18 Oct	Autumn Retreat	PH	Steve and Sandra Piggott
16 Oct	Women's Autumn Day	WAH	Lynn Penson
19 Oct	Facing Dashed Hopes and Shattered Dreams	WAH	Chris Ledger
24 Oct	Preaching Seminar	WAH	Andy Peck
25–27 Oct	Women's Weekend	PH	Lynn Penson
30–31 Oct	Dealing with Discord in Schools	WAH	Hilary Turner and Liz Mole

Please also pray for students and tutors on our ongoing **BA in Counselling** programme at Waverley and Pilgrim Hall and our **Certificate and Diploma of Christian Counselling** and **MA in Integrative Psychotherapy** held at London School of Theology.

For further details and a full list of CWR's courses, phone +44 (0)1252 784719 or visit the CWR website at www.cwr.org.uk Pilgrim Hall: www.pilgrimhall.com

Health for the soul

FOR READING & MEDITATION – EXODUS 3:1–12

'"... When you have brought the people out of Egypt, you will worship God on this mountain."' (v.12)

Today we reflect on the second time the word 'worship' is mentioned in Scripture. God tells Moses that the first thing the children of Israel must do when they have been delivered from Egypt is to worship Him. This begs the question 'Why does God want His people to worship Him?' Well, one answer is because worship is the right response to God as He is. When great mountaineers are asked 'Why do you want to climb Everest?' they reply 'Because it is there!' So it is with worshippers. We worship God because He exists and because He is who He is – the great Creator God.

FURTHER STUDY

Psa. 8:1–9; Psa. 43:1–5

1. What caused the psalmist to worship?

2. How did the psalmist speak to his soul?

Again the emphasis is that just as it is natural to feel awed by the sight of a beautiful sunset so it is natural to respond to the Creator's beauty and goodness in spontaneous praise. There is something unusual about a person who is drawn to the ugly and repelled by the beautiful. Perhaps that is why C.S. Lewis, in his book *Reflections on the Psalms*, wrote, 'Worship is inner health made audible'.* Those who feel unable to enter into worshipping God live impoverished lives; their souls are unhealthy because the soul is designed to function best when it is in touch with its Creator – when it reaches out to Him in an attitude of praise and worship. One sign of spiritual dis–ease in a Christian is that he or she has no desire to worship. Such Christians have perhaps become self-centred rather than God-centred.

Worship, then, is not only the right response to God but is healthy for the soul. We function best when our souls reach out to our Creator in worship and praise. There can be no health in the soul if there is no worship in the soul.

O Father, just as I long for physical health so I desire health for my soul also. I accept that I am made in order to worship. May I do so not merely as a duty but with delight. In Jesus' name. Amen.

'He is everything'

FOR READING & MEDITATION – EXODUS 10:21–29

'"Our livestock too must go with us ... We have to use some of them in worshipping the LORD our God ..."' (v.26)

If you search a concordance you will discover that between the passage we looked at yesterday and the one we have read today the word 'worship' is mentioned more than ten times. Clearly Moses had grasped the fact that the worship of God by the Israelites was of prime importance. There could be no real health in the nation of Israel without worship.

C.S. Lewis, whose writings are so good on the subject of worship and praise, makes the point that there can be no real life in the soul, no completeness in the personality, if true worship of God is absent. He says that to worship God in spirit and in truth is 'simply to be awake, to have entered the real world'.* Failure in worship results in spiritual poverty. It again re-emphasises: no worship, no spiritual health.

In Egypt the children of Israel were impoverished not only physically, but spiritually also, by their lack of worship. Now, however, all that is to be changed. They are to learn that the God they may have thought of as 'Something' is now to be 'Everything' to them. *Everything*.

Apparently when the great conductor Toscanini had finished conducting a brilliant performance of Beethoven's 5th Symphony the audience leapt to their feet, applauding wildly and shouting their delight. Toscanini waved his arms equally wildly, imploring those who were cheering to stop. As soon as they did he turned to the orchestra and shouted hoarsely, 'You are nothing!' Next he pointed to himself and said, 'I am nothing!' Then he cried, 'Beethoven is everything, everything, everything!' That, in effect, is what we do when we worship God. When we worship we are saying, 'He is everything, everything, everything.'

FURTHER STUDY

2 Sam. 23:13–17; 1 Chron. 29:10–20

1. How did David divert devotion for himself to God alone?

2. What did David acknowledge?

O God my Father, without reservation or hesitation my heart responds in the same way: You are indeed everything. Everything! Blessed be Your holy name. Amen.

* C.S. Lewis, *Reflections on the Psalms*, copyright © C.S. Lewis Pte. Ltd. 1958. Used by permission.

MON
9 SEP

Celebrating His victory

FOR READING & MEDITATION – EXODUS 15:1–8

'... "I will sing to the LORD, for he is highly exalted. The horse and its rider he has hurled into the sea."' (v.1)

We look now at the very first song recorded in the Bible – as we are discovering a natural, spontaneous response to the amazing miracle of deliverance from Egyptian tyranny. Having arrived safely on the other side of the Red Sea, Moses leads God's people in an exuberant celebration, and the Exodus is celebrated in a magnificent hymn of praise. So the children of Israel praise God not only because He exists but also because of what He has done for them in rescuing them from slavery in Egypt.

The song begins by proclaiming God as *the warrior* (v.3) who has fought for the Israelites against their enemies and overcome them. From this point on in Scripture the marching songs of the children of Israel celebrate *God's* 'military prowess', not theirs. They are the battle hymns not of a republic but of a kingdom, and focus on God's presence as the guarantee of success. It is interesting to note that elsewhere the Exodus is presented as a victory not just over Pharaoh but also over the gods of Egypt (Exod. 12:12). In this sense it was a battle fought and won in the spiritual realm.

FURTHER STUDY

Luke 2:8–14; Rev. 5:9–14

1. What did the angels celebrate?
2. What did the heavenly throng celebrate?

In recent years there has been teaching in the Christian Church on the subject of spiritual warfare which advocates attacking Satan with words of praise about God. Nowhere that I am aware of is this found in Scripture. Praise is not a weapon to be directed at the devil; praise is the lifting of the hearts towards God. The archangel Michael, when disputing with the devil, did not resort to praise. He confronted the devil with these words: 'The Lord rebuke you!' (Jude v.9). To celebrate God as Creator and Redeemer with conviction and faith is to proclaim His victory over everything. His victory–always His remember, not ours.

My Father and my God, what comfort it gives me to know that there is nothing that cannot be overcome when I stay close to You. You have conquered everything. In You I, too, can be a conqueror. Amen.

Priming the pump

FOR READING & MEDITATION – EXODUS 15:9–12

'"You stretched out your right hand and the earth swallowed them."' (v.12)

We can learn a lot about praise and worship by examining the composition of this spontaneous outburst of praise sung by the Israelites. The song goes on to rejoice not only in God's power but also in His *uniqueness* (v.11): 'Who is like you – majestic in holiness, awesome in glory, working wonders?' The Israelites' praise proclaims the fact that the God who creates and redeems and triumphs is incomparable.

Whenever you are at a loss for some reason to praise God, think of His resurrection, all that He has accomplished for you, and the fact of His uniqueness. There is no one on earth or in heaven, who can be compared to Him. This is something which certainly helps me as I consider His great love for me. The pattern laid down in the Song of Moses and Miriam is one that we would do well to study closely and follow.

It helps to remind ourselves that the reason we have been delivered from 'Egypt and slavery' is in order to worship God. Sir Herbert Butterfield, the Cambridge historian, said of the Exodus, 'I know of no other case in history where gratitude was carried so far, no other case where gratitude proved to be such a generative thing ... It gave the children of Israel a historical event that they could not get over, could not help remembering and, in the first place, it made them historians – historians in a way that no one had been before.' But Israel's deliverance is as nothing compared to what God has done for us in Christ. If Israel could not get over such a physical deliverance then how can we ever get over such a spiritual deliverance? The answer is that we will never get over it either here or in eternity.

FURTHER STUDY

Isa. 40:25–31; Eph. 1:3–14

1. How can our faith and enthusiasm be renewed?
2. What historical event helped Paul?

Gracious Father, as I think about what You have done for me in Christ, not only do I realise that I can never get over it but also that I never want to get over it. Your deliverance is the best thing that has happened to me. Amen.

'You're not home yet!'

FOR READING & MEDITATION – EXODUS 15:13-18

'"The LORD will reign for ever and ever."' (v.18)

Because the God who has redeemed Israel is the Creator of the whole world, this first song sung by the children of Israel also emphasises the universal Lordship of the Almighty over every nation. The shock waves created by the Exodus are felt by all the nations affected by this act of God – they tremble with fear at the prospect of the conquest of Canaan (vv.15–16).

Illustrated a few days ago was the fact that the victory was God's, and God's alone; it is reinforced here by the statement that it was not God's army that accomplished the Exodus but His strong and mighty arm (v.16). Yet this warrior God is also the God of unfailing love who leads His people home (v.17). Here the song prophetically anticipates the conquest of Canaan and the building of the Temple. And it closes with the triumphant acclamation that the Lord will reign for ever and ever.

FURTHER STUDY

John 14:1–7;
Heb. 11:8–16

1. What is Jesus preparing?

2. What was Abraham's longing?

Can I ask you to consider this: God is the God of the whole world and His love will always lead His people home. Of course, for the Israelites 'home' was the land God had promised them. For us 'home' is heaven. C.S. Lewis once wrote, 'Our Father refreshes us on the journey with some pleasant inns but will not encourage us to mistake them for home.'*

A missionary tells of returning by ship to his home country. As he watched people disembark and walk into the arms of their loved ones who were expecting them he grew somewhat saddened because he realised that there was no one there to welcome him. Rather petulantly he said to his heavenly Father, 'Why couldn't You arrange for me to have someone to welcome me home?' The Lord whispered, 'You're not home yet.'

O Father, help me never to forget that this world is not my home. I'm just passing through. And may I rejoice in the knowledge that when I do reach home You will be there to greet me. All honour and praise be to Your name for ever. Amen.

Do you want to dance?

FOR READING & MEDITATION – EXODUS 15:19–21

'Then Miriam ... took a tambourine in her hand, and all the women followed her ...' (v.20)

The awareness of the great deliverance which the children of Israel had experienced in being rescued from Egypt leads Miriam to take a tambourine and dance, whereupon all the women follow her example and sing and dance before the Lord.

At this point in the story those of us who are Westerners tend to explain this conduct away as Middle Eastern exuberance. However, if this is our only reaction we should pause and ask ourselves: Do we ever get so excited about our deliverance from sin's bondage that we want to dance? 'Dance?' you might exclaim. 'Really dance? I thought it was just our hearts that were to "dance at the sound of His name".' The commentator Walter Brueggemann says about this section of Scripture, 'The news is borne and enacted by the women who dance ... towards freedom. For a long time they had not been able to dance – too tired, too fearful, too intimidated. God had acted to save and their dancing was a way of asserting they were daughters of Yahweh's freedom.'

As we explore various expressions of Christian joy it is all too easy to feel superior and respond, 'Well, you would never catch me dancing in a Christian meeting'. And that may be true, but do you not sometimes feel like dancing when you reflect on what God has done for you in Christ? The indwelling of the Holy Spirit imparts an awareness within us that all is well with our soul. It makes music inside of us. Exuberance and devotion can go hand in hand. Church history bears witness to that. People often dance or jump with joy when they hear some sensationally good news. Well, you'll never hear better news than the news of what God has done for you in Jesus.

FURTHER STUDY

Psa. 149:1–9; Psa. 150:1–6

1. In what does God delight?

2. How are we to praise God?

My Father, I know that what the Bible says about dancing cannot be made into a doctrine, but whether I dance or not, help me to know in my heart the presence of Your joy that will at least make me feel like doing so. In Jesus' name. Amen.

Four aspects of worship

FOR READING & MEDITATION – EXODUS 24:1–18

'... the people ... responded with one voice, "Everything the LORD has said we will do."' (v.3)

We linger a little longer in the book of Exodus to consider this vivid narrative in which God's covenant with Israel is dramatically confirmed. From this episode we can discover at least four basic aspects of worship. First, it is important to note that God convenes the meeting. It is the Father who invites His people to gather to meet Him as the assembly of the Lord. When Moses gives God's directions, the people respond with one voice and agree to do things God's way (v.3). This suggests to us that worship is God's calling to us and is to be conducted on His terms. In other words, worship is led by God's terms, not by our temperaments.

Second, the story tells us that in worship different people have different roles to play, so participation is the keynote. Third, the meeting involved listening and responding to God's Word. Without this, worship is incomplete (vv.3,7). No worship service is worthy of the name if it does not strengthen our understanding and obedience to God's Word. Fourth, in worship the community is engaged in the renewal of the covenant, so the 'covenant book' is read (in our case, the Bible) and the 'covenant blood' is poured out (for us, the cup of communion). Our relationship with God is sealed and our worship made valid by blood sacrifice (vv.6,8).

Of course, much has changed because of the sacrifice of Jesus – not least that every worshipper can now come near to a holy God and has no need to worship at a distance (see v.2). But the other aspects we have noted are still valid. So remember this: in corporate worship we are called by God, everyone is to participate, and the Word of God must be central – and all this because of the shed blood of Jesus.

FURTHER STUDY

2 Kings 23:1–3, 21–25; Acts 2:42–47

1. How did Josiah follow the four aspects of worship?

2. How did the Early Church follow these principles?

Father, may these four important features become an integral part of our corporate times of worship. Help us not to miss one of them for we want our worship to be nothing less than complete. In Jesus' name. Amen.

Water-carriers
in a dry and thirsty land ...

Jesus said, 'If anyone is thirsty, let him come to me and drink' (John 7:37). And we are all thirsty people, longing for God to revive and refresh us.

God is opening new doors and a new chapter for CWR. We are embarking on a new and exciting journey, enabling teachers to pour out God's love and to be a godly influence in their chosen vocation. Join us as we invest in the provision of Continuing Professional Development and Initial Teacher Education, grounded in a biblical worldview.

Please help CWR to invest in building a generation of people who are strong in character and grounded in biblical truth.

Please fill in the 'Gift to CWR' section on the order form at the back of this publication, completing the Gift Aid declaration if appropriate.

Enjoy!

FOR READING & MEDITATION – DEUTERONOMY 12:1–14

'There, in the presence of the LORD your God, you and your families shall eat and shall rejoice ...' (v.7)

On our travels through the Old Testament we can only pause here and there to observe what Scripture reveals to us about worship. Today we dip for a moment into the book of Deuteronomy, and we see in the passage before us that the children of Israel are commanded when they enter the Promised Land not to worship the Lord their God in the way that heathen people worship their gods. They are to have one central place of worship, and when that place is revealed to them they are to worship and rejoice. The Lord encourages them not to enter into worship simply as a duty but as a delight. Worship that has no delight in it is not true worship.

John Piper frequently makes reference in his writings to the fact that although we do not worship God in order to experience joy, the inevitable consequence of worship is finding deep joy and satisfaction for our souls, including emotional release and wholeness. Piper says, 'Where feelings for God are dead, worship is dead.' Some Christians teach that worship is giving to God and that we ought not to indulge ourselves in the positive feelings that the Spirit stirs within us as a result. Although it is wrong to worship God purely in order to experience joy, there is nothing wrong with enjoying the feelings that flow into our hearts as a consequence of worship.

Theologians throughout the ages have said that our destiny is not only to work for God but to enjoy Him also. The more you give your mind and thoughts to Him the more joy will fill your heart. There is therefore no need to deny those feelings or attempt to smother them. They are the inevitable result of worship. So enjoy!

FURTHER STUDY

Luke 10:18–24; John 15:9–11

1. What is the basis of our rejoicing?

2. What were among Jesus' characteristics?

Gracious Father, I see there is a mutual ministry at work when I worship. You enjoy me, and I enjoy You. Help me not to regard my worship as a duty but always as a delight. In Jesus' name. Amen.

Songs we still sing

FOR READING & MEDITATION – 1 CHRONICLES 15:1–24

'... David ... prepared a place for the ark of God and pitched a tent for it.' (v.1)

This incident, taken from the book of Chronicles, sheds further light on this intriguing subject of worship. David's actions seem astonishingly bold. He leaves the tabernacle of Moses, with its animal sacrifices and priesthood, at Gibeon, and erects another tent in Jerusalem. There, once the dedicatory offering had been made, only the non-sacrificial worship of praise and prayer operated. This was an amazing innovation which lasted forty years until Solomon built the Temple and fused Davidic praise with Mosaic ritual.

Often David's action is seen as a prophetic one illustrating that praise which lies beyond animal sacrifices in the kingdom of God. From this time on the worship in David's tabernacle provided the pattern for the conduct of worship in Israel. It was David's tabernacle, we should note, that gave birth to the psalms (cf. 1 Chron. 16:7–36). David's arrangements for the establishment of praise in the new tabernacle in Jerusalem make for challenging reading. Worship was not a disorderly free-for-all. It was led by those who had consecrated themselves to this sacred task (v.12), and were committed to God's way of doing things (v.13). Musical skill and training were encouraged and were not seen as a denial of spirituality (v.22). The priority was joyful singing to balanced musical accompaniment (v.16) – not, as is so often the case in some circles, characterised by feeble singing drowned out by overamplified music!

So rich and true was this worship introduced in Old Testament times that its songs, if not its tunes, have lasted for 3,000 years. The truths expressed in the psalms of David are with us today. We sing them still!

FURTHER STUDY

Psa. 23:1–6; Acts 15:12–19

1. Why have David's songs proved everlasting?

2. How was David's tent prophetic of the Church?

Gracious and loving Father, the more I consider my spiritual heritage the more praise rises in my heart. Thank You for all that has gone on before. I am rich in You because others were rich in You. Amen.

'No flags at half mast'

FOR READING & MEDITATION – 1 CHRONICLES 15:23–29

'... Israel brought up the ark of the covenant ... with shouts, with the sounding of rams' horns and trumpets ...' (v.28)

Yesterday we saw that when David established the new form of worship in Jerusalem he wanted everything to be done in a considered and thoughtful, as well as a joyful, way. But he knew that what mattered above all was the presence of God in worship, and this was symbolised by the ark of the covenant. Nothing else really mattered. The ark was the wooden box covered with gold which had once stood in the Most Holy Place in the tabernacle. It was the visual symbol of God's presence, and regarded as the earthly footstool of His heavenly throne.

David knew the ark had been neglected in Saul's reign (1 Chron. 13:3) and was determined to restore it to its central place in worship. The king was so exuberant about this that he stripped off his royal outer garments and, clothed in a linen undergarment like a priest, led the procession into the city in an unselfconscious dance of joy. Not for the last time did someone find such exuberance offensive and unbecoming. David's response to his critical wife is that he will become even more undignified than this if it means celebrating the Lord's presence with His people (cf. 2 Sam. 6:21–22).

As we said the other day, people express themselves in different ways in worship – some dance and others do not. But the great C.H. Spurgeon's advice surely applies to us all: 'Never hang your flag at half mast when you praise God! No, run up every colour, let every banner wave in the breeze, and let all the powers and passions of your spirit exult and rejoice in God your Saviour.' Surely even the most restrained among us should consider this! If worship doesn't get to your feet then at least let it get to your heart. Remember: no flags at half mast!

FURTHER STUDY

Isa. 29:13; Rev. 3:14–22

1. How did people praise God at half mast?

2. How might a church have its flags at half mast?

O God, help me I pray to enlist every joyful emotion that runs through my heart in expressing my appreciation for what You have done through Jesus Your Son. Let all my spirit exult and rejoice in You. In Jesus' name. Amen.

The 'Amen mentality'

TUES
17 SEP

FOR READING & MEDITATION – 1 CHRONICLES 16:1–6,36

'Then all the people said "Amen" and "Praise the LORD."' (v.36)

Worship in Old Testament times was most certainly a multi-media event! No one, we imagine, ever fell asleep in David's tabernacle – at least not while the songs rang out, cymbals clashed, trumpets sounded, and the harps and lyres were strummed. But everything was done with a clear purpose.

As we see from verse 4, the priestly leaders were appointed to do three things: first, to make petitions to the Lord; second, to thank God by publicly acknowledging what He had done; third, to praise God and extol His name. The musicianship of gifted people supported the offering of praise. It was in this atmosphere that some of the best known psalms originated – as the two examples given in this chapter indicate.

Notice also that when the psalms had been sung all the people said 'Amen' and 'Praise the LORD'. How important it is in corporate worship to cultivate this 'Amen mentality'. Not every worshipper takes part in everything at every moment, but everyone is expected to participate by being attentive and worshipful and by being willing to give ready assent to all that is offered. Corporate worship is not the sum total of many individuals 'doing their own thing', as we say, but involves all of us affirming the faith we share as the people of God in joyful and wholehearted agreement.

Sunday worship would be revolutionised if there was more response from the congregation, especially in those churches which do not use a liturgy. How rich and heart-warming it is when the people of God give a hearty 'Amen' to the truths enunciated in His presence.

FURTHER STUDY

2 Cor. 1:15–22; Rev. 19:1–8

1. In what sense is Jesus the amen of God?

2. What characterises worship in heaven?

Father, forgive us that often we are so slow to respond to truth either with a vocal 'Amen' or even with a silent 'Amen' in our hearts. May we not take Your blessings for granted but accept them with gratitude. In Jesus' name. Amen.

Worth singing about

FOR READING & MEDITATION – 1 CHRONICLES 16:7–22

'Glory in his holy name; let the hearts of those who seek the LORD rejoice.' (v.10)

As we have observed over the past couple of days, the major innovations David made in the new tabernacle in Jerusalem gave rise to some of the collections of psalms. The ancient historian shows us this by placing at this point in his narrative two typical psalms – Psalm 105:1–15 and Psalm 96.

The first song, for which Asaph is the spokesman, celebrates the unique identity of Israel among the nations. The psalmist sings first of God's *miraculous power* which redeemed Israel from slavery and created a people to glorify His name (vv.8–13). God's people owe everything to God – to the wonders He has performed on their behalf.

The song also heralds the *marvellous promises* of God (vv.15–18). God's people have good reason to praise Him when they consider His ability and eagerness to keep His promises. In this particular instance God is praised for the redemptive promises He kept which He had made with Abraham centuries before. Remember always that we worship a covenant-making and covenant-keeping God. We, it seems, can so easily forget our promises but He *never* forgets the ones He has made.

FURTHER STUDY

Psa. 105:1–15; Psa. 118:1,13–29

1. How does Psalm 105 reinforce and reinvigorate faith in God?
2. What is the basis of our thanksgiving?

Lastly, the prophetic singer rejoices in the *miraculous protection* God has afforded the Israelites (vv.19–22). Throughout their history God had protected and preserved them and thus shown that they were His anointed ones – His chosen people. The Israelites had something to make a song and dance about. So also do we. This soul-redeeming, promise-keeping, protecting God of the Old Testament is the same today. What He is He was, and what He was He is, and what He was and is He ever will be. Amen.

Yes, my Father, with all my heart I say it: 'Amen' and 'Amen'. Not one of Your promises has ever been broken. I want to bless and praise Your holy name for ever. Amen.

Bowing before beauty

FOR READING & MEDITATION – 1 CHRONICLES 16:23–36

'For great is the LORD and most worthy of praise; he is to be feared above all gods.' (v.25)

The second sample psalm, on which we focus today, can be found also as Psalm 96. How wonderfully it illustrates the extraordinary range of worship in the Bible. What God has done for His people demands the attention of all the earth (v.24). The first psalm (vv.7–22) had celebrated the mystery of Israel – a special nation whose existence can only be explained by supernatural power and promises and protection. The song we are looking at now heralds the message which Israel has to tell to the nations. The very existence of the Israelites as a worshipping people demonstrates the unique and timeless glory of God. To declare this God as the one true God is to dethrone all the idols of the other nations (vv.25–26).

Israel also exists to declare God's present rule. All the families and nations in the world – indeed, the joy-filled heavens and trembling earth – are recruited to share the happy conviction that 'the LORD reigns' (v.33). Notice the invitation in verse 29. In the parallel verse (Psa. 96:9) Eugene Peterson paraphrases this as 'Bow before the beauty of God' (*The Message*). When God's people enter into worship there is a sense in which their hearts surrender to His overwhelming attractiveness. As we said earlier, the more we know of God the more attractive He becomes to our souls. Finally, the song turns our eyes and hopes towards God's future coming (v.33). Even while we rejoice in God's present kingship we relish the prospect that one day He will come to fully establish His kingdom of justice.

These three dimensions of God's Person and work fuel our thanksgiving and praise (vv.34–36) and evoke a hearty 'Amen'.

FURTHER STUDY

Psa. 96:1–13;
Psa. 27:1–14

1. What did the psalmist desire?
2. What are we to proclaim?

My Father and my God, my heart does not hesitate to bow before Your beauty. I rejoice in the kingdom You are building now and also in the one to come. Thank You that I have an inheritance in both. Amen.

Introduction to Biblical Care and Counselling

'Changed and transformed from the inside out, I feel enthused, excited and equipped to go on and serve the Lord in new ways.'

This was just one of the responses from recent attendees at our Introduction to Biblical Care and Counselling course (IBCC). The five-day IBCC course is a well-proven opportunity not only for learning how to help others effectively, but also for developing an understanding of ourselves – an experience that one delegate described as 'a journey of self-discovery'. Designed for people from all walks of life with a heart to help others, the course will better equip participants to play a part in the lives of those who are struggling, enabling them to grow into the person God desires them to be.

God-centred teaching is led by experienced tutors from the CWR team, through whom participants learn the biblical basis for pastoral care and counselling, together with a framework for the counselling process. The course will lead to a clearer understanding of why problems develop and how to help those experiencing them, and it also lays foundations to develop further counselling skills.

The IBCC is ideal for all those looking for basic training in pastoral care, those in full or part-time ministry, leaders of small groups, and anyone who wants to help people in their everyday lives or is thinking of embarking on full counselling training. On completion of the course, there is an opportunity to undertake further training with Waverley's Certificate of Christian Counselling or by enrolling on the BA (Hons) Counselling degree leading to an award from Roehampton University.

Courses are regularly available at both of the CWR training centres – Waverley Abbey House, set in spacious lakeside grounds in Farnham, Surrey and Pilgrim Hall, set in twelve acres of beautiful grounds in Uckfield, East Sussex. The undisturbed peace and beauty of both venues offer a wonderful environment for learning and personal reflection. Join others who have found that this course is a 'life changing experience [which] opens your eyes to God's character and His perfect plans and purposes.'

The next available courses are
Mon-Fri 18-22 November 2013
at Waverley Abbey House, or
Mon-Fri 17-21 March 2014 at Pilgrim Hall.

For more information or to make a booking, call **01252 784719** or visit **www.cwr.org.uk**

Prophetic praising

FOR READING & MEDITATION – 1 CHRONICLES 25:1–8

'David ... set apart some ... for the ministry of prophesying, accompanied by harps, lyres and cymbals.' (v.1)

Buried deep in the historical books of the Old Testament are thoughts and ideas that are worth more than gold when it comes to understanding biblical worship. Here, with an historian's eye for detail, the chronicler records how David had arranged for worship to be conducted. Though there is room, as we shall see, for spontaneity, most of the activity related to worship was thought through. This did not make it unspiritual. Quite the contrary.

What is especially interesting about this passage is that it shows that praising God is essentially a prophetic activity. To prophesy in the Old Testament is nearly always to speak out God's word. There is foretelling, of course, but there is much more forthtelling – speaking out God's message both in word and in song. Do you realise, therefore, that when you sing out your praises to God you are acting prophetically?

Remember this also: when we worship we are doing much more than merely expressing a passing mood. In singing songs which have a credal and gospel content we are prophetically declaring the truth of what God has done and said. We are prophetically proclaiming how great and good and gracious God is and what He has achieved. What is more, through praise we prophetically celebrate not only what God is doing among us now but what He plans to do in the future too. We sing of His past salvation, His present rule, and His coming kingdom. And because our praise is truly prophetic we help to bring about what God has promised and planned. This is why nothing should ever take the place of worship in the Christian Church. Nothing.

FURTHER STUDY

2 Kings 3:9–20; Luke 1:67–79

1. How are music and worship linked to prophetic ministry?

2. How did Zechariah combine praise and prophecy?

O Father, the more I explore the subject of worship the more my heart realises how much more we, Your people, need to understand in our worship of You. Help us dear Father. In Jesus' name. Amen.

Spiritual warfare

FOR READING & MEDITATION – 2 CHRONICLES 20:1–29

'... "Give thanks to the LORD, for his love endures for ever."' (v.21)

This story of how Jehoshaphat defeated Moab and Ammon teaches us some more important lessons about praise and worship. Prepared by prayer and fasting, and emboldened by God's promise that the battle is His and not theirs, Jehoshaphat, king of Judah, sends out singers as his front-line troops.

But look at what they sing. They do not sing these songs at the enemy – a point we made earlier – as if praise were a spiritual weapon. These songs are not targeted at the opposition but offered to God in worship. The songs they sing are not martial songs calling down defeat on the enemy. On this occasion they do not even sing of the Lord's power or might. No, they sing boldly of the unfailing love of God – that covenant love with which God is committed to His people.

In many ways, praise is faith set to music. It expresses our confidence in a God who has already won the decisive battles. The way to face the devil when you feel you are a victim of his attacks is not to lash back at him, albeit in God's name, with angry denunciations. Simply declare boldly that the Lord loves you, keeps His covenant with you, and will never forsake you. The fight we have in nearly every case of fear and danger is the fight of faith – or indeed, for faith. It is the struggle to maintain our confidence in Jesus at all costs. Nothing strengthens faith more in such circumstances than to join in the chorus of defiant praise: 'God is indeed good, and His covenant love lasts for ever.' But remember: by praising we do not so much fight the battle as proclaim the victory of our God. This more than any other single thing is the secret of spiritual warfare.

FURTHER STUDY

Josh. 6:8–20; Psa. 8:1–9

1. What was the role of the musicians at Jericho?

2. How does praise silence God's enemies?

Father, help me learn this lesson for I see that it is based so solidly on Scripture. Help me to rely on You whenever I feel under attack and not on human techniques or strategies. In Jesus' name. Amen.

An Old Testament revival

FOR READING & MEDITATION – 2 CHRONICLES 29:1–36

'Hezekiah and all the people rejoiced at what God had brought about for his people ...' (v.36)

The revival that took place under Hezekiah saw the restoration of all that was best about worship in the Old Testament. It reinstated many of the features of Israel's worship which we have already mentioned.

Not surprisingly, the worship had to be re-established in the way prescribed by David (v.25), and under prophetic direction. Clearly, it was also a priestly activity which was led by the Levites (v.26) who were consecrated (v.34). Sacrifice was at the heart of it too (vv.27–35). The shedding of blood at the Passover, which marked the nation's original deliverance, was continued in the regular animal sacrifices at the tabernacle and then at the Temple. Later we will note how this was both reaffirmed and radically redefined by the once-for-all sacrifice of Jesus on the cross.

Consider now the fact that in the revival of true worship under Hezekiah singing was a prominent feature (vv.27–30). The songs sung were those composed by or dedicated to David and so almost certainly included some of the psalms that we know (v.30). The music was lively and varied, although we can only imagine how it sounded! The praise was lyrical and expressed gladness (v.30). It was vocal and it was physical, involving kneeling and bowing the head. The worship scene we are looking at today was one that impacted all the senses, affected the whole personality, and involved the whole assembly (v.28).

Surely the worship of God enacted at the time of the revival under Hezekiah represents the high-water mark of Old Testament worship. Should not Christian worship today at least be equal to, if not surpass, it?

FURTHER STUDY

2 Chron. 5:12–14; 2 Chron. 35:10–19

1. What happened when worship started in the Temple?

2. Where were the musicians during Josiah's Passover?

O Father, forgive us that sometimes our Christian worship does not even equate to Old Testament worship. We have so much more to be grateful for. Forgive us and help us. In Jesus' name. Amen.

The highest form of worship

FOR READING & MEDITATION – JOB 1:6–22

'At this, Job ... tore his robe ... Then he fell to the ground in worship ...' (v.20)

As we journey through the Old Testament we come to what is considered by many to be one of the oldest books in the Bible. What a picture the opening words of this book give us of a man's determination to worship God no matter what his circumstances.

Satan, we are told, came before God and said, 'Does Job fear God for nothing? ... stretch out your hand and strike everything he has, and he will surely curse you to your face' (Job 1:9,11). Satan is given permission to interfere in Job's life, and one day, like a bolt out of the blue, tidings of disaster shook him to the core. Hot on the heels of one another come the messengers of woe. The reports are devastating. His oxen and donkeys have gone, his sheep and camels have gone, his servants have gone, his children have gone. With a single stroke he has lost almost everything. But think of the moral splendour of this: Job, hearing the numbing news, falls on the ground and *worships*.

How many of us, in similar circumstances, would have responded in this way? Clearly Job possessed the conviction that God was to be worshipped not only because of what He does but also for who He is. As we have already discovered, one part of worship involves giving God praise for what He has done for us, but the purest form of worship is worship that is given to God just for who He is. It is easy to worship God when everything goes right; it is not so easy, however, when everything goes wrong. It all goes back to what we were saying earlier about the issue of trust. Job trusted God and believed that He had good reasons for allowing what had happened. And we say again: that kind of trust means we offer the purest form of worship.

FURTHER STUDY

Hab. 3:1–19

1. How did Habakkuk regard God?
2. How did he view the day of calamity?

O Father, how I long to develop a trust in You that is as deep as that of Your servant Job. Bring me to that place in my Christian life I pray. Please, dear Lord. In Jesus' name I ask it. Amen.

Justifying God's goodness

FOR READING & MEDITATION – PSALM 22:1–11

'O my God, I cry out by day, but you do not answer ... Yet you are enthroned as the Holy One ...' (vv.2–3)

We move now into the book of Psalms. This book, more than any other book in the Bible, takes us to the depths of worship and praise and was, as you may be aware, the hymn book of the ancient Israelites.

The song on which we are concentrating today gives the lie to the suggestion (as we saw with Job) that worship is possible only when things are going right. Far from it. Worship is not a superficial response to the blue skies and fairness of life. Often we discover the Bible's richest worship is a cry of praise from the depths and from the darkness. It is the God-forsaken, it is also interesting to note, who affirm that God is 'enthroned' on the 'praise' of His people (v.3).

How can we continue to celebrate our trust in a God who is always right in a world where often so much is wrong? Worship in times of darkness is the defiant answer of faith to praise God if not for everything then certainly *in* everything. As the great theologian G.C. Berkouwer memorably said, 'The remarkable fact is that all the questions that arise in Scripture around what we call the problem of theodicy [a term used for arguments which justify God's goodness in a world where evil exists] have their profoundest and most definitive answer in a "hallelujah!"' He went on, 'The wonder is that the paeans of praise arise so often in hard times, that the songs are heard so frequently from the shadow, and that the doxology is sung as the last candle-light of life's joy flickers.'

We glorify God by continuing to give Him praise and worship even when our circumstances might seem to deny His goodness.

FURTHER STUDY

Acts 16:16–34; James 5:7–11

1. How did Paul and Silas express defiant faith and what resulted?

2. Why should we consider Old Testament Job?

O Father, help me to bless Your name even in the midst of pain and suffering or happenings that some might call 'calamities'. Others have done this and with you, so can I. In Jesus' name I pray. Amen.

We know His name

FOR READING & MEDITATION – PSALM 29:1–11

'Ascribe to the LORD the glory due to his name ...' (v.2)

Worship and praise, as we have been discovering, is the appropriate response to all that we know about God. We worship Him for many reasons, among them the fact that He exists and that He has done so much. In the psalm we have read today the psalmist draws our attention to another reason why we ascribe glory to God: because of His *name*.

Christians are not like the Athenians who erected an altar 'TO AN UNKNOWN GOD' (Acts 17:23). We know God's *name*. As you are aware, a relationship is transformed when we are able to call a person by their name. God has revealed Himself to us as a personal God who can be known personally and loved and worshipped. Our praise, therefore, is not something that is unfocused – a shot in the dark; it centres on His name. One of the key acclamations of the Bible is 'Hallelujah' (translated in our Bibles as 'Praise the LORD', eg Psa. 106:1,48). The word is made up of two parts: 'hallel' (to praise) and 'yah' or 'yahweh' which is God's covenant name, made known to Moses at the burning bush when He declared 'I AM WHO I AM' (Exod. 3:14). Jesus took that great mysterious name of God and linked it to simple things that we can understand when He said, 'I am the gate' (John 10:7), 'I am the light' (John 8:12), 'I am the good shepherd' (John 10:11), 'I am the way and the truth and the life' (John 14:6).

Biblical worship has many facets, one of them being a joyous celebration of the fact that God has revealed to us His name – a name that demonstrates and introduces us to His reliability, faithfulness, love, mercy, deliverance, power and compassion. How wonderful! How truly wonderful.

FURTHER STUDY

Matt. 1:18–25; Acts 4:8–12

1. What was significant about the baby's name?

2. What did Peter explain?

Father, how can I thank You enough that I do not worship an 'unknown' God? I know Your name and You know mine. All honour and glory be to Your name for ever and ever. Amen.

THURS
26 SEP

The most important thing

FOR READING & MEDITATION – PSALM 34:1–22

'Glorify the LORD with me; let us exalt his name together.' (v.3)

In this psalm we are urged to *glorify* the Lord and exalt His name together. Glorifying God is our number one priority when we gather together to worship the Lord.

The theologian Donald McCullough says, 'What we do on Sunday mornings ... the order of events and the manner in which we enact the drama ... must always point to God, must reinforce again and again that God has taken the initiative and called us together, that God's grace is more important than our sin, that God's will is more important than our desires, and that God's glorification is more important than our edification.' We should not take that last sentence to mean that our edification is unimportant; what he is saying is that God's glorification is more important. To lose sight of that is to lose sight of one of the main purposes of the Church. Those responsible for leading ought always to have a keen eye for ensuring that God's name is glorified in every single thing that is done.

In the late 1990s, Matt Redman wrote the song *The Heart of Worship*. It contains a thought that should always be present in our hearts when we come together to worship, which is that our worship should always be just about Jesus. It should never be about ourselves.

It was written at a time when people in Matt's church were reflecting on being producers in worship rather than consumers and the words flowed from a new perspective of worship being all about Jesus. How might our services pulse with the energy of the Spirit if our worship, too, was centred only on glorifying the name of Jesus?

FURTHER STUDY

Psa. 86:1–17; Rom. 15:1–7

1. How did David glorify God in the midst of trouble?
2. How can we glorify God?

Lord Jesus, help us to approach every worship service with the attitude that it is not about us – it's all about You. And help us also not to pay lip-service to our words but to apply them to every part of our lives. Amen.

Serving the Church in South East Asia

CWR has long been committed to serving the Church worldwide and we recognise that God has opened doors for us in various regions; most noticeably in recent years in Singapore, Malaysia and South East Asia. Through relationship and a number of 'God-incidences', we have been able to provide regular teaching and resources.

In SE Asia this year, by God's grace, we have been able to run a range of courses from Insight Days to weekend and week-long seminars and biblical counselling training. We have also made available *Every Day with Jesus for New Christians* in Mandarin.

We are hoping to offer fully accredited Christian counselling programmes in early 2014, in response to the need identified by church leaders in the area. Work has also begun on translating and exploring distribution for more resources in Mandarin.

We would greatly value your prayers and support for this area of CWR's ministry as we seek to know, understand and outwork all that God has given us to do.

On being real

FOR READING & MEDITATION – PSALM 88:1-18

'Why, O LORD, do you reject me and hide your face from me?' (v.14)

Today we continue reflecting on this important issue of lament. The book of Psalms, as stated earlier, was the hymn book of the people of God. The psalms were sung publicly in the same way that we sing our modern hymns. But what do you think would happen if the psalm before us now was set to music and sung in your church next Sunday? Can you imagine people singing, 'But I cry to you for help, O LORD ... Why, O LORD, do you reject me and hide your face from me'? But honestly, aren't there times when you feel like that? Sadly, many Christians respond to their negative feelings by pretending they do not exist. By doing so they think they are being spiritual, but actually they are ducking into denial. Integrity involves facing whatever is true.

Yesterday we made the comment that lament is 'praise offered in a minor key'. We do not much like the minor key. We prefer our songs to be upbeat and joyful. Walter Brueggemann says, 'There is an enormous temptation for "high faith" to deny the dark side of life when things do not work ... against that common failure the psalms of lament make contact with the emotions of failure.' We seem to be as afraid of lament as we are of catching a serious case of the flu. Why is this? Is it because we fail to see that openness and honesty is the soil out of which grow true confidence and joy?

The ancient Israelites sang their songs of lament as worshipfully as they sang their hymns of praise. They were able to express their emotional struggles as part of their worship, knowing that God would not turn His face away from them. God delights in our passionate engagement with Him, and what He longs for is that all His children be real.

FURTHER STUDY

Psa. 142:1–7; Prov. 25:20; Luke 22:39–44

1. Why might exuberant worship be unreal?

2. How did Jesus engage with His Father?

O Father, I long among other things to be a real person. Help me not to dodge issues or run down the path of denial. Teach me how to face and feel my negative feelings yet without losing my confidence in You. In Jesus' name. Amen.

When God becomes real

FOR READING & MEDITATION – PSALM 89:46–52

'How long, O LORD? Will you hide yourself for ever?' (v.46)

If all of the 150 psalms included in the book of Psalms – the spiritual hymn book of Israel – focused only on joy then they would not be true to life. In fact, a close examination of the book of Psalms shows that psalms of complaint, confusion, doubt, and heartache significantly outnumber the psalms that focus on joy.

Though denial, as we saw yesterday, causes us to gloss over the negative feelings that may from time to time arise within us, the verses in which the psalmists express lament help us to acknowledge them. John Calvin, the sixteenth-century Reformer, said, 'The psalmists lay open their inmost thoughts and affections and call, or rather draw, each one of us to the examination of himself in particular in order that none of the infirmities to which we are subject and of the many vices in which we may abound may remain concealed.'

The writer of the psalm before us today cries, 'How long, O LORD? Will you hide yourself for ever?' Don't you feel as you read those words that the psalmist is battling with some deep-seated emotions? He is being ruthlessly honest, however, as he seeks to be as real as it is possible to be. We don't know for sure but it is possible that the psalmist's natural instinct was to pretend that he was not feeling the way he was. Whether or not that was the case, honesty and integrity caused him to look into the depth of his soul and admit to his true feelings.

We need never be afraid of expressing our real feelings in God's presence: the more real we are with God the more real we will discover Him to be.

FURTHER STUDY

1 Kings 19:1–18; 2 Cor. 1:3–11

1. How did Elijah engage with God?

2. What real feelings did Paul express?

O Father, may I never be afraid of expressing my real feelings – of crying out from the depths, so to speak. Help me understand that to reach the depths in You I must first be willing to reach the depths in me. Amen.

Open the door

FOR READING & MEDITATION – PSALM 103:1–22

'Praise the LORD, O my soul; all my inmost being, praise his holy name.' (v.1)

As we begin a new month it may be that the meditations of the past few weeks which have stressed the importance of worship have made some of you who are struggling with serious and pressing problems feel a little threatened. Perhaps you are saying to yourself, 'When I go to church my problems seem to overwhelm all other thoughts and make it difficult for me to concentrate on giving God praise. If the truth be known, I am more interested in finding solutions to my problems than focusing on praise.' If that is the way you feel and you are willing to admit it then full marks for honesty!

A once-popular song by Bruce Ballinger urges us to forget about ourselves and concentrate on worshipping Him. This is easier said than done when life is filled with problems. But though it is not an easy thing to do, it is not impossible. In the psalm we are looking at today the psalmist seems to be holding a conversation with his soul. He talks to his soul and says in effect, 'Come on, soul. Do what you are supposed to do and begin to praise the Lord.' Although it is true, as we have been saying, that worship and praise is our response to God, there are times when our soul is in a state of spiritual idleness and so we need to take the initiative and begin to praise Him – even though we may not feel like it.

God has made each and every one of us choosing beings, so the next time you don't feel like worshipping you can choose to do so anyway. You may find, as thousands before you have found, that the door you open to God in your soul is the door through which He comes to renew you and refresh you.

FURTHER STUDY

Psa. 42:1–11; Acts 5:40–42

1. Identify the emotions and attitudes of the psalmist.
2. How did the apostles respond to a flogging?

Gracious Father, You have made me with the ability to choose. Help me use that ability in the service of my soul. When I am next tempted to give way to self-pity may I vote against my feelings and give You the praise You deserve. In Jesus' name. Amen.

Holy reality

FOR READING & MEDITATION – JEREMIAH 7:1–15

'Do not trust in deceptive words and say, "This is the temple of the LORD ..."' (v.4)

Often the Old Testament prophets come across as being very serious and severe and sometimes what they say doesn't make for comfortable reading. That is one reason why many steer clear of the Old Testament. As Christians we live in two Testaments – the Old as well as the New. In the interests of truth we must look, therefore, at a prophetic exposure of false worship.

In the passage before us today we see Jeremiah at the very gate of the Temple denouncing the inconsistency between the people's way of life and their way of worship. The prophet's sermon attacks the practice of worshipping in the Temple while outside its confines the poor are being ill-treated (v.6). Dietrich Bonhoeffer, the Lutheran pastor executed by the Nazis, famously challenged the Church in Germany, which at that time was blind to the persecution of the Jews, with these words: 'Only those who cry out for the Jews have the right to sing Gregorian chants.' There were those in the Temple at Jerusalem – especially the ruling élite – who no doubt thought Jerusalem was inviolable, and that God would protect His people no matter how cynical and corrupt they became. They needed to be reminded of the truth that judgment begins with the family of God (see 1 Pet. 4:17). Though the worship centre at Shiloh had once been a dwelling-place for God's name, God had destroyed it, and Jerusalem would suffer the same fate (v.12). 'The Temple,' says Walter Brueggemann, 'had become a means of cover-up for the destructive way life is lived in the real world.'

True worship is a meeting with holy reality. Our lives are only as rich as our worship, and our worship is only as rich as our lives.

FURTHER STUDY

Isa. 58:1–14

1. What was inconsistent about God's people?
2. What should they do?

Father, hold me steady once again as I face this burning issue. I must ask myself: How authentic is my life? Do my lips equate with my life – and vice versa? Help me give an honest response to this. In Jesus' name. Amen.

First things first

FOR READING & MEDITATION – HOSEA 2:8–15

'"... she decked herself with rings and jewellery, and went after her lovers, but me she forgot," declares the LORD.' (v.13)

We look now at another Old Testament prophet who emphasises the issue raised yesterday, namely that acceptable worship is inseparable from acceptable living. Hosea condemns the way Israel had adopted the culture of Canaan and, in particular, was assimilating the worship of the local pagan god, Baal.

'Baalism' was tailored to the human desire for health, wealth and prosperity. In fact, Baal was a prosperity god whose worship was meant to guarantee fertility and success. The worship of Baal was highly sensual and even included prostitution. It was designed to arouse religious feelings. Commenting on some Western worship Eugene Peterson says, 'The phrase "Let's have a worship experience" is really Baalism's substitute for "Let us worship God."' Prostitution, or harlotry, took place in a physical sense but also became a metaphor for spiritual fornication, that is, worship equated with 'whoreship'. To quote Peterson again: 'Baal worship sought fulfilment through self-expression, worship that accepted the needs and passions of the worshipper as raw material. "Harlotry" is worship which says: "I will give you satisfaction. You want religious feelings? I will give them to you. You want your needs fulfilled? I'll do it in the form most attractive to you."'

FURTHER STUDY

Isa. 1:1–23

1. Why did God reject people's worship?

2. What should they do?

We must be careful that we do not import into our worship the attitudes of the culture of our day. The spirit of the age leads us to crave excitement and seek sensations. In this 'therapeutic culture', as it has been called, people often want to be either entertained or soothed and stroked and made to feel better about themselves. Is that what we seek when we gather to worship together?

O Father, forgive us if we have imported into our worship the culture of our day. We know that there is comfort to be found in You, but help us put You first and our own needs last. In Jesus' name. Amen.

Half-baked Christians

FOR READING & MEDITATION – HOSEA 7:1-10

'Ephraim mixes with the nations; Ephraim is a flat cake not turned over.' (v.8)

The way in which a wrong concept of God destroys a person's spiritual life is seen most dramatically in the life of Ephraim – one of the tribes of Israel. There was a time when God was the sole object of the worship of those belonging to this tribe. Hosea tells us in 13:1, 'When Ephraim spoke, men trembled; he was exalted in Israel. But he became guilty of Baal worship and died.' Hosea is referring here to the fact that in the beginning Ephraim was a powerful tribe from which came the great leader Joshua. Now, however, Ephraim is charged with having turned from serving the true God and bowing the knee to an idol – Baal.

You can be sure that didn't happen all at once. The change would have come gradually. Perhaps the people became more interested in men's opinion than in God's. Or perhaps pride took over and they started to usurp God's position. One thing is sure: the moment they allowed the picture of God to be changed in their minds their life started to disintegrate. Listen to this: 'When Ephraim saw his sickness ... [he] turned to Assyria' (Hosea 5:13). Their own power gone, they align themselves with the strongest power of the day.

FURTHER STUDY

Psa. 78:9–22; Hosea 13:1–6

1. Describe the men of Ephraim.
2. Identify the stages of Ephraim's decline.

Ephraim could be understood as those half-baked Christians who have a part of their lives turned towards God and a part to the world. The danger is decay quickly sets in. One of the most important things we can do to maintain a strong spiritual life is to ensure that we keep close to the picture of God presented in the Scriptures. Once we allow ourselves to 'make God in our own image' our lives quickly start to fall apart. Stay close to Scripture. Study it regularly. It will teach you all you need to know about God and how He is to be worshipped.

Father, forgive me if the picture I have of You is one I have conjured up rather than one drawn from Your revelation of Yourself in Your Word. Guide me into truth – the truth about You. In Jesus' name. Amen.

When God doesn't show up

FOR READING & MEDITATION – AMOS 5:21-27

'I hate, I despise your religious feasts; I cannot stand your assemblies.' (v.21)

As we continue in these meditations we remind ourselves that we are using the word 'worship' in its broadest sense to cover the whole of life's response to God. If nothing else, this sharply reminds us that we cannot sincerely join in the public praise of God if our daily lives are being lived in direct contradiction of His commandments.

In today's reading we find that though the worship services are crowded, the singing enthusiastic, and the offerings lavish, the worshippers' daily lives are corrupt and ungodly and they are oppressing the poor and needy. Amos bravely exposes the form of worship that was masking unethical behaviour. God will not tolerate such hypocrisy, he says. When people meet in God's name pretending to worship Him, one thing is sure: God doesn't turn up! As Alec Motyer puts it, 'Their worship was dutiful, exceedingly costly – think of the outlay on animals for sacrifice – apparently whole-hearted, emotionally satisfying, but if religion does not get through to God it has failed centrally.'

One of the worship centres used by the Israelites was at Gilgal (4:4). Ironically, Gilgal had gained its name from the time when God had rolled away their reproach (Josh. 5:9). Now the people were not 'holy-rollers' but 'unholy-rollers'! If there's any 'rolling' to be done now, says Amos, let it be the 'rolling down' of the river of God's pure justice to clean up society (v.24). True worship depends not on how loudly we sing or on the musical competence of the worship team. Rather, it depends on how clean our hearts are. As it's been said 'Acceptable worship is inseparable from acceptable living.'

FURTHER STUDY

Psa. 15:1–5; Psa. 24:1–10

1. Why should we keep our word even if it hurts?

2. What is required of a true worshipper?

Gracious and merciful God, give us clean hearts so that when we approach You our worship is truly in spirit and in truth. Help us see that unless we are living correctly we cannot worship correctly. In Jesus' name. Amen.

'True God of true God'

FOR READING & MEDITATION – MATTHEW 2:1–12

'... "Where is the one who has been born king of the Jews? We saw his star in the east and have come to worship him."' (v.2)

It is time now to start exploring the New Testament to discover some of the things we can learn about worship. In the passage before us today we come across the very first reference to the word 'worship' in the New Testament Scriptures. We read that Magi, or Wise Men, from the east, having seen a strange star in the heavens and having recognised it as a sign that the Son of God had come to earth, travelled to Jerusalem to worship Him.

It's interesting to me that though the ancient seers of Israel had strained their eyes in the darkness and caught a glimpse of the fact one day God's Son would visit this earth, the first to tell of the fulfilment of those prophecies were not Jews but Gentiles. As one Bible commentator says, 'This time Magi forestalled Israel who possessed the clear prophetic word.' We can only speculate as to what went on in the minds of the Magi as they looked down on the Christ child. Did they realise that the young child before them would change the nature of worship for ever?

The Jews affirmed their belief in one living God. 'Hear, O Israel,' they said over and over again, 'the LORD is one.' By implication this meant that all other 'gods' were imaginary deities. The birth of Jesus revealed that there is a second Person in what we now call the 'Trinity' – someone who is equal to God, who, like Him, is eternal, and who has been with Him from the beginning. There was a time when Jesus became man, but never a time when He became God. He was man from the manger but God from all eternity. And when we bow before Him and worship Him we are worshipping One who is God. In the words of the Nicene Creed, 'true God of true God'.

FURTHER STUDY

John 1:1–18; 10:30–33

1. Compare and contrast Jesus and John.

2. Why did the Jews try to stone Jesus?

Father, it is difficult for our human minds to understand this great mystery that to worship Jesus is to worship You. But though we cannot understand it, we stand upon it. I bring You my worship once again today. In Jesus' name. Amen.

WED
9 OCT

The urgent and the important

FOR READING & MEDITATION – LUKE 10:38–42

'"... but only one thing is needed. Mary has chosen what is better, and it will not be taken away from her."' (v.42)

We touch now on the lives of Mary and Martha - an illustration that underlines that though we can worship God through our work, we must be careful that we do not become devoted to our work and make it all-important. It is perilously possible to become more interested in what we do than in for whom we are doing it.

Martha, bustling about her business in the home, began to complain when she saw that her sister Mary was sitting at Jesus' feet and listening to Him rather than helping to get things done. Jesus, with deep insight and understanding, quickly distinguishes between what we might call the urgent and the important. Mary, said Jesus, was doing the better thing – engaging with Him rather than just doing things for Him.

How easy it is to become more interested in working for the Lord than being with Him in worship. Don Bjork, a Christian writer, points out that the Great Commission was given to worshipping people. Matthew records, 'When they saw him, they worshipped him ... Then Jesus came to them and said, "All authority in heaven and on earth has been given to me. Therefore go and make disciples of all nations, baptising them in the name of the Father and of the Son and of the Holy Spirit ... "' (Matt. 28:17–19). Unless we are closely involved with Jesus we have little to offer to a needy world. It is so easy, as many have found to their cost, to become more taken up with the work of God than with God Himself, more enamoured with the cause of Christ than with Christ Himself. Be careful that you do not allow the urgent to crowd out the important. Nothing is more important than spending time with Him in prayer.

FURTHER STUDY

Acts 6:1–7; Rev. 2:1–7

1. What did the apostles realise?

2. How did the Ephesians do what was urgent but not important?

O Father, save me I pray from making my work the be-all and end-all. May I never become so engrossed in what I am doing that I fail to engage directly with You. In Jesus' name I pray. Amen.

Worship – repentant praise

FOR READING & MEDITATION – LUKE 17:11–19

'"Was no-one found to return and give praise to God except this foreigner?"' (v.18)

How astonishing: ten lepers were healed by Jesus but only one returned to give thanks! From this incident in the life of Jesus it is possible for us to draw a number of lessons.

Being 'cleansed' from our sin is, of course, the basic ingredient in order to connect with God, but we must never forget the purpose for which we are cleansed – to give Him worship and praise. When one of the ten lepers 'saw he was healed' he realised the extraordinary miracle that had occurred and wanted to give Jesus thanks for it. He alone, we are told, turned round, came back, praised God, and threw himself at Jesus' feet to show his appreciation of what the Saviour had done for him. Only then, and only to this one returning worshipper, did Jesus say, 'Rise and go, your faith has made you well' (v.19).

At the risk of overstating the point, the goal of salvation is not that we are cleansed or healed but that we return to God in humble service and heartfelt worship. P.T. Forsyth expressed it like this: 'The Christian life is repentant praise.' It consists of ongoing repentance, not in the sense of a perpetual wallowing in our guilt or sinfulness but in a continual returning to God in praise and thanksgiving. Worship is really regular repentance.

Follow the pattern presented in these verses and you will not go far wrong: keep coming back to God with passionate and exuberant praise ('a loud voice', v.13), with deep submission ('threw himself at Jesus' feet', v.16), and joyful thanks (v.16). We can be cleansed, healed, restored, forgiven, but it is not until we return all the way back home in praising and glorifying God that we are made whole.

FURTHER STUDY

Exod. 36:1–7; 1 Chron. 17:1–2

1. How did the people express thankful, repentant praise?

2. What was David's concern?

Father, I am awed by the fact that You have saved me, but help me never to forget that the purpose of my salvation is to glorify You. I do so now. In Jesus' name. Amen.

A time now come

FOR READING & MEDITATION – JOHN 4:1-26

'Yet a time is coming and has now come when the true worshippers will worship the Father in spirit and truth ...' (v.23)

Today we pick up on the words of Jesus in which He says that the Father seeks *worshippers*. And so the main focus of our meditations is now made by Jesus Himself. It could be said that Jesus came to seek and to save the Father's lost worshippers. This one Samaritan woman, who had sought to satisfy her deep spiritual thirst possibly through sexual fulfilment, comes 'thirsty' to the well. There she meets the One who has living water to offer – water that will satisfy her parched heart and end her relentless search for inner peace and happiness.

A new thought is introduced by Jesus into the concept of worship: we are saved in order to worship the Father 'in spirit and truth'. God is Spirit, and we worship Him properly when we are in a *spiritual* relationship with Him. To worship 'in spirit' is explained by George Beasley-Murray in this way: 'The worship that God seeks is not frozen to a sacred building ... or tradition but a worship which is living, the ever new response to God who is Spirit as prompted by and enabled by the Spirit of God.'

FURTHER STUDY

Mal. 1:6–14; Acts 2:42–47

1. Why were offerings not in truth?

2. Where did early Christians worship?

If that is what is meant by worshipping 'in spirit' what does it mean to worship 'in truth'? Well, it means so much more than worshipping sincerely because it is possible to be sincere but sincerely wrong. To worship 'in truth' is to offer worship that is rooted in knowledge, in contrast to the Samaritan woman's ignorance (v.22). It is worship based upon the reality which is revealed in Jesus Christ who is Himself the truth. A new day has dawned, said Jesus. The time has come when no longer does worship depend on sacrifices or rituals. We are free to worship God anywhere and everywhere.

O Father, my gratitude knows no bounds when I realise that I have been born in a time when You are to be worshipped 'in spirit and truth'. This is a day of good tidings. I will rejoice in it and be glad. Amen.

Every Day with Jesus
One Year Bible

Out of habit and for no other reason, we quite often turn to sections of the Bible we are familiar with, missing out on a deeper and far more satisfying insight and revelation of God's Word that is meant for each one of us.

The good news is the release during August of the new NIV edition of the much loved *Every Day with Jesus One Year Bible*, which presents portions of the Old Testament, the New Testament, Psalms and Proverbs, brought right up to date with the use of the 2011 NIV text. So, there is plenty of variety that is easily read in fifteen minutes or less each day.

Life-related devotionals selected from Selwyn Hughes' inspirational writing tie directly into suggested prayers and further study sections, helping to apply God's Word to the readers' lives, enriching their experience as they dig deeper and learn in both a regular and practical way.

For details of how to use this resource as part of the new *Every Day with Jesus* Church Challenge - which has to be one of the most exciting and rewarding journeys church members can take together by reading the Bible in a year - register your church to receive a FREE welcome pack. This includes posters, invitations and bookmarks - plus a generous bulk discount on your Bibles. To register, visit **www.cwr.org.uk**

To purchase this Bible, priced at £19.99, visit www.cwr.org.uk/store or a Christian book shop.

SAT
12 OCT

Partnership in the Godhead

FOR READING & MEDITATION – JOHN 20:24–31

'Thomas said to him, "My Lord and my God!"' (v.28)

We can only speculate as to exactly when the disciples realised that their teacher was none other than God in human form. They certainly had good reason to believe He was greater than any other person they had known: the winds were obedient to His commands, multitudes were healed of their illnesses, and He was able to send demons fleeing with a single word. Three of the disciples once saw Him positively transfigured (Matt. 17:1–8).

The disciples would no doubt have been deeply impacted by the fact that Jesus could bring the dead back to life and offer people the forgiveness of their sins. And, as some teachers of the law so rightly remarked, 'Who can forgive sins but God alone?' (Mark 2:7). He said, 'Anyone who has seen me has seen the Father' (John 14:9), and 'I and the Father are one' (John 10:30). Did the full weight of who He was really dawn on them while He walked with them in the Galilean and Judean hills?

Some think a complete understanding of who He was came only after the resurrection. Perhaps, oddly enough, it was Thomas who showed that he realised more clearly than the others that Jesus was not merely a mortal adopted to divinity when He said, 'My Lord and my God'. Did Thomas mean by 'God' all that we mean when we use that term? Surely it must have been so. Suddenly Thomas came to see that there is partnership in the Godhead, that in worshipping the Son He was worshipping One who was equal to the Father. If Jesus was not God His integrity would have led Him to say to Thomas, 'I am not who you say I am'. The fact He did not is yet another great testimony to the truth of His deity.

FURTHER STUDY

John 5:16–18; 14:1–14

1. What motivated the Jews to kill Jesus?

2. What did Jesus explain to Thomas and Philip?

Father, once again we are at the central mystery of our great and most holy faith. One God yet three in one. God above us, God among us, God within us. We bring our worship to You, great and mighty triune God. Amen.

Communion thanksgiving

FOR READING & MEDITATION – 1 CORINTHIANS 11:17–34

'... and when he had given thanks, he broke it and said, "This is my body, which is for you; do this in remembrance of me."' (v.24)

The words we have read lead our minds back to what many refer to as the Last Supper: 'The Lord Jesus ... took bread, and when he had given thanks, he broke it ...' How remarkable these words are. When they were first uttered, Jesus was on the verge of making His final self-sacrifice. In effect Jesus gave thanks for His own self-offering! In doing so He was drawing together important Old Testament threads, for thanksgiving in Israel was expressed not only through public praise but through sacrificial offering (cf. Lev. 7:12; Psa. 50:23). The ultimate 'thank offering' – and the final sin offering – was the offering of Jesus Christ to His Father on the altar of the cross.

Not surprisingly, it is from the Greek word for 'giving thanks' (*eucharisteo*) that we derive the term for our commemoration of His sacrifice – 'the Eucharist'. If any, this thought of thanksgiving could be uppermost in our appreciation of the Communion service. It would save us a great deal of controversy if we concentrated less on the elements (the bread and wine) and more on the actions involved. After all, Jesus instructed, 'Do this in remembrance of me.' It is the actions which are significant – the taking, breaking, eating, drinking. And at the heart of this commemoration is the giving of thanks. The realisation of this might well transform our times of Holy Communion.

The Eucharist, or the Lord's Supper, is a celebration – a festival, not a fast; a resurrection feast, not a funeral wake. At the table of Communion we share in the Church's great out-pouring of gratitude and praise for the one great act by which Jesus hallowed the Father's name and glorified His Father's holy nature.

FURTHER STUDY

Acts 27:33–37; 1 Cor. 10:16–17

1. What was Paul's habit?

2. How did he think of communion?

Blessed Lord Jesus, how can I thank You enough for bringing God to me and bringing me to God? The next time I am at the Communion table deepen my thinking and my appreciation of my actions I pray. Amen.

'A central mystery'

FOR READING & MEDITATION – 2 CORINTHIANS 13:11–14

'May the grace of the Lord Jesus Christ, and the love of God, and the fellowship of the Holy Spirit be with you all.' (v.14)

Now that we find ourselves in the epistles we can begin to see what is so distinctive about Christian worship. We can sum it up in one word: it is Trinitarian. The worship of the New Testament churches dramatically expresses their conviction that God is a Trinity of love – Father, Son and Holy Spirit.

Earlier we said that it was Thomas who first gave expression to the idea that there is partnership in the Godhead. After the Holy Spirit came at Pentecost all the disciples realised that love, power and authority are not the prerogatives of the Father and the Son only – the Spirit also possesses them and is a co-equal partner in what we now call 'The Blessed Trinity'. The great doctrine of the Trinity has not been fashioned, as someone has said, 'to make a simple thing difficult for ordinary people and thus help theologians to maintain their mystique'. It arose from the experience of the Early Church. The apostles said in effect, 'We have come to know much more about God. Now we see that He has a Son who is equal to Him, and that the Holy Spirit, who is also an equal partner, takes the things of the Son and reveals them to us. We cannot fully explain the Trinity, but there is no doubt that when we refer to it we are speaking of the central mystery of our most holy faith.'

FURTHER STUDY

Matt. 28:16–20; Acts 5:1–11; 2 Cor. 3:12–18

1. How is the Holy Spirit regarded as God?

2. What did Peter explain?

From the earliest years of the Church the threefold blessing given in our text for today has been in use. We can never repeat it or use it enough, for every time we do the expression deepens the impression: God is one, but one in three and three in one – Creator, Redeemer, Sanctifier. The Father in majesty, the Son in suffering, the Spirit in empowering. Once again let us adore the great triune God.

Father, Son and Holy Spirit, my heart rises in worship to You. Though I cannot fully fathom the mystery, my heart is loyal to the truth. I rejoice in who You are, great and mighty triune God. Amen.

Completing the circle

FOR READING & MEDITATION – EPHESIANS 1:1–6

'Praise be to ... God ... who has blessed us ... with every spiritual blessing in Christ.' (v.3)

The point we are to think about is one that we have touched on before, but now we shall consider it in more depth: our praise and worship actually blesses and brings pleasure to God.

The apostle Paul here launches a great outpouring of praise to his heavenly Father which begins with the words 'Praise be ... ' The NKJV text here reads 'Blessed be ... ' a more specific translation of the Greek word *eulogeo*, which means 'to bless'. But please don't let this translation divert you from the point that Paul is making: God blesses us and we bless Him in return! In William Hendrickson's words, 'Gratitude is that which completes the circle whereby blessing returns to the Giver in the form of unending adoration.' In their book *Doxology* Daniel Hardy and David Ford express the thought in this way: 'Blessing is the comprehensive praise and thanks that returns all reality to God, and so let's all be taken up into the spiral of mutual appreciation and delight which is the fulfilment of creation.'

Paul goes on to bless God as the Father of all the blessings that have been lavished upon us as part of His eternal plan (vv.5–6). You might be interested to know that in the Greek Paul's words from verse 3 to 14 actually form one long sentence. It is a veritable volcano of praise, marked by great intensity and effusiveness – the piling up of extravagant language that perfectly matches his mood of wonder and thankfulness to God. Paul is clearly beside himself as he reflects on the fact that all believers have been blessed in the heavenly realms in Christ. The simple truth Paul wants us to grasp is this: the reason why God should be blessed is because He has blessed us.

FURTHER STUDY

Gen. 12:1–13; 14:18–20; Acts 3:1–10

1. How was Abram part of a circle of blessing?

2. How were Peter and John part of a circle?

O Father, it is such a privilege, so to speak, to complete the circle. You have blessed me and now I bless You. I would never have come to You unless You had come to me. For that I am eternally grateful. In Jesus' name. Amen.

Relishing the blessings

FOR READING & MEDITATION – EPHESIANS 1:7–14

'... that we, who were the first to hope in Christ, might be for the praise of his glory.' (v.12)

Yesterday we saw how the apostle Paul, in the opening sentences of Ephesians, ascribes blessing to God – something that was an Old Testament tradition. Since he was an apostle of Jesus Christ, however, it is not surprising to find him, having given praise to the Father for His loving and eternal plan, now celebrating the fact that all God's saving initiatives centre on Jesus. God's sovereign will and grace are worked out in Jesus. 'Blessed be the God and Father of our Lord Jesus Christ,' he is saying, 'whose eternal and heavenly will has ushered in the historic events which occurred in Bethlehem and at Calvary.' God's eternal intentions have become saving actions in Christ. That's worth a 'Praise the Lord' isn't it, even before we come to our usual prayer of thanks at the end?

Let's together enjoy the blessings that come to us from the Father through Jesus. Bless Him for our 'redemption through his blood' (v.7) – we have been set free because Jesus has paid the ransom price for us. Bless Him for 'forgiveness' (v.7) – that moral miracle by which our guilt is assuaged, the slate is wiped clean and, no longer condemned, we have new hope in Christ. All that comes from God and Christ flows to 'the praise of his glory' (v.12). Bless Him, too, that all these blessings have been made effective in our lives by the Holy Spirit (vv.13–14). Every movement of the Spirit's work also contributes to 'the praise of his glory' (v.14).

This is what the commentators Daniel Hardy and David Ford call 'the ecology of blessing'. In this ecosystem of love, the love which flows out of God to us and back to Him again in loving praise and worship is the love that makes the world go round.

FURTHER STUDY

Psa. 31:1–11;
Rev. 1:1–8

1. Who are blessed?

2. What blessings does John identify?

O God of wisdom and love, I bring to You my heartfelt appreciation and praise. Help me be a witness to Your wisdom and love as I go about my tasks this day. In Jesus' name. Amen.

Abba, Father

FOR READING & MEDITATION – EPHESIANS 2:11–18

'For through him we both have access to the Father by one Spirit.' (v.18)

True worship envisages every tribe and tongue and nation drawing near to God through Jesus Christ. What unites Jew and Gentile – those near and those far away – is the reconciling work of Jesus on the cross. Jew and Gentile can now enjoy equal access to the Father through Jesus who died and rose again, and this is made effective in the Spirit.

New Christians often ask the question: Should our worship be directed to God the Father, God the Son or God the Spirit? Worship is ultimately *to* the Father, *through* the Son, *in* the Spirit. This is not to say that we cannot ascribe honour directly to Jesus; indeed, we can and we must. Nor does it mean that we can never directly ascribe praise to the Holy Spirit as God; we can and may, when appropriate, invoke the Holy Spirit personally. It is, however, to say that even when we do give equal honour to the Son and to the Spirit we are, at the same time, giving glory to the Father (cf. John 5:23; Phil. 2:11).

Our sense of security in worship comes from three things: first, knowing God as our Father; second, coming to Him in the assurance that He receives us because of the work accomplished by His Son on our behalf at the cross; third, from Christ's continuing intercession for us at God's right hand. But let's not overlook the great work of the Spirit in all this. Paul reminds us in one of his earlier letters – the letter to the Romans – that the Spirit testifies to us inwardly that we are God's children, and this witness in our hearts causes us to cry '*Abba*, Father' (Rom. 8:15). In this 'magnetic field of the Holy Spirit' we can find ourselves being drawn to praise even when we might not really feel like it.

FURTHER STUDY

Rom. 8:3–17; 1 Cor. 2:9–16

1. How can we be close to God?

2. How can we understand God?

Father, I am so thankful that Your Spirit is at work in my heart persuading me to praise You even when my feelings might cause me to remain silent. Let that ministry of the Spirit in my heart be ever there I pray. In Jesus' name. Amen.

FRI
18 OCT

God's earthly address

FOR READING & MEDITATION – EPHESIANS 2:19–22

'And in him you too are being built together to become a dwelling in which God lives by his Spirit.' (v.22)

Our praise and worship which, as we have been saying, is our response to who God is and what He has done for us, is offered through Jesus or in His name. To fully understand this we need to explore more of what Jesus had to say about the Temple. Clearly Jesus loved the Temple at Jerusalem because on one occasion He drove out the money-changers saying, '"My house will be called a house of prayer for all nations." But you have made it "a den of robbers"' (Mark 11:17). Yet He knew that one day He Himself would replace the Temple so that people would no longer need a building in which to worship God (see John 2:19–22). He did this in two ways.

First, in Jesus' day the Temple was the place of sacrifice for sins. Jesus displaced the Temple by the offering of Himself as the ground of our acceptance by God. In David Peterson's words, 'Jesus offers the sacrifice that inaugurates the new covenant, fulfilling and replacing the system of worship associated with the Mosaic covenant. The pure worship He offers to God ... is the only basis on which we can find acceptance and draw near to God.'

Second, the Temple was the location of the focused presence of God. Jesus displaced the Temple by His resurrection body. By the life which He imparts to those who are in Him they are formed into a living temple of God in the Spirit. In every act of worship we experience afresh the miracle of the coming of the risen Jesus to be with His followers. Coming together in Christ's name in the Spirit we form 'a dwelling in which God lives by the Spirit'. Be staggered at it if you will but the worshipping Christian Church is really God's earthly address.

FURTHER STUDY

1 Cor. 3:16–17; 6:15–20; 1 Pet. 2:4–10

1. Where does God live?

2. What makes worship acceptable to God?

O Father, how thrilling it is to experience afresh in every corporate worship service the miracle of Your coming into our midst. You are not only seated on Your Father's throne but present when we praise You. How wonderful. Amen.

NEXT ISSUE

EVERY DAY WITH JESUS
Nov/Dec 2013

Love Came to Bring us Home

When Adam and Eve sinned, they were expelled from Eden. But although God expelled them, He did not abandon them.

This issue encourages us to take a realistic view of life. Until we see God in heaven, we must live out our lives 'East of Eden' in a land of thorned resistance. But we are shown how to deal with the difficulties we encounter and use them to strengthen our faith. We can persevere, focusing on the God who has planned everything for us.

- Learn to trust God whatever your circumstances
- See how Christ is working in your life
- Experience the comfort of the Holy Spirit

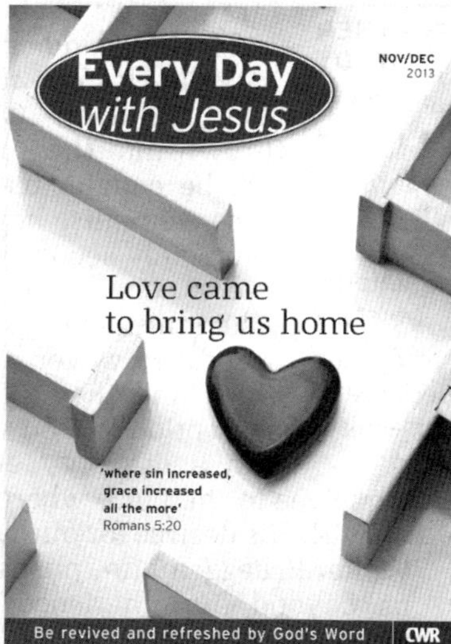

Also available as eBook/ eSubscription

OBTAIN YOUR COPY FROM
CWR, a Christian bookshop or National Distributor.
If you would like to take out a subscription, see the order form at the back of these notes.

SAT
19 OCT

'Life at full stretch'

FOR READING & MEDITATION – EPHESIANS 3:14-21

'Now to him who is able to do immeasurably more than all we ask or imagine ... to him be glory ...' (vv.20–21)

In today's reading we see Paul ascribing 'glory' to God and offering what we describe as a 'doxology'. This word comes from the Greek word *doxa* which means 'glory'. Glorifying God involves a leap of faith because we are affirming our confidence in a power and a person higher than our own. To worship is to cast ourselves adoringly into the arms of a God '... who is able to do immeasurably more than all we ask or imagine'. This is why worship has been described as 'life at full stretch before God'. When we worship we are taken out of ourselves. We do not fall into a trancelike state but transcend our own thoughts and feelings and centre our souls on God.

Daniel Hardy and David Ford also say in their book *Doxology*, 'Our whole life is continually thrown into the air in praise in the trust that it will be caught, blessed, and returned renewed.' Once we realise how much God loves us and how completely secure we are in Him then we are set free to concentrate on God in thanks and praise. When this happens all sorts of growth and change occurs. However, they are by-products and not aims, and they flourish in our unselfconscious absorption in God who is the object of our praise.

In a doxology of praise we are lifted out of ourselves to the place where we enjoy God and are caught up with His desires for our world. Doxology, in the words of Walter Brueggemann, 'pushes us beyond control, summons us beyond our cherished rationality, rescues us from anxiety, transcends despair, overrides arrogance, strips us of self-sufficiency, and leaves us unreservedly and entirely entrusted to this Other One who cares for us more than we care for ourselves.' That says it all, does it not?

FURTHER STUDY

1 Sam. 10:1–7; Psa. 138:1–8

1. What would happen to Saul when he encountered worship?
2. What was the experience of the psalmist?

Gracious God and Father, may my heart be a constant doxology of praise that lifts me out of myself and into closer contact with Yourself. May my life always be 'at full stretch'. In Jesus' name. Amen.

Word and Spirit

FOR READING & MEDITATION – EPHESIANS 5:1–20

'Do not get drunk on wine ... Instead, be filled with the Spirit.' (v.18)

The deeper we go into the subject of what constitutes Christian worship the more we realise how dependent we are on the work of the Holy Spirit within us to reach God. The Word of God is a powerful ingredient to praise, but so too is the Spirit.

In the passage before us now Paul urges us to 'be filled with the Spirit'. In making the contrast between being drunk with wine and being filled with the Spirit the apostle is contrasting life in the Spirit with the Ephesians' pagan past. Nevertheless, he is clear: the Spirit's presence is again the needed ingredient for worship and praise. From what is known about worship in the churches Paul founded, biblical scholar Gordon Fee has concluded that it was 'free, spontaneous worship ... apparently orchestrated by the Spirit Himself'. Dr Martyn Lloyd-Jones suggested that: 'as the result of the operation of the Holy Spirit upon us, worshipping God is no longer a matter of duty, it is a desire'.

When Christians are open to both the Word of God and the Spirit, the Word and the Spirit combine in a dynamic way, and this provides for the rich variety in worship expressed in what Paul describes as 'psalms, hymns and spiritual songs' (v.19). It is not easy to draw fine distinctions between these three but I would suggest the following. 'Psalms' may have been Old Testament psalms sung with Christian insight and understanding; 'hymns' may have been newly composed hymns to Christ; 'spiritual songs' were probably songs offered in worship at the prompting of the Holy Spirit. How much richer and more varied might our worship be when we open ourselves to the Word and the Spirit through 'psalms, hymns and spiritual songs'?

FURTHER STUDY

Acts 2:1–18; 10:44–48

1. How did people view the Spirit-filled disciples?

2. What happened when people spoke the Word of God?

O God, save us from being satisfied with worship that lacks Spirit-inspired dynamism and variety. Lead us on to deeper and richer worship we pray. In Jesus' name. Amen.

Total reliance on the Spirit

FOR READING & MEDITATION – PHILIPPIANS 3:1–11

'For it is we who are the circumcision, we who worship by the Spirit of God, who glory in Christ Jesus ...' (v.3)

We continue exploring Paul's epistles in our quest to increase our understanding of Christian worship. You may wonder what the passage before us today has to do with worship, especially the text chosen which talks about circumcision. Well, consider this: we are able to worship God because we are the true members of God's covenant family. Paul's shorthand for this idea is 'circumcision' because from the time of Abraham onwards circumcision had been the sign of belonging to God's covenant people. So Paul is assuring his Christian readers in the church in Philippi that they are covenant people, the 'true circumcision'. In the new covenant we know the joy of sins forgiven, and because we have been forgiven much, we love much.

Under the old covenant only the priests were allowed to approach God, but now all believers can draw near to Him. Thus we worship with confidence and joy. Those who belong to the new covenant 'boast in the Lord' (2 Cor. 10:17). And why do we 'boast'? Listen to Dr Martyn Lloyd-Jones on this point: 'True believers boast in Christ Jesus, they exult. They not only believe on Him but their whole being is moved as they contemplate Him ... they want to boast of the greatness and the wonder and the glory of the Person of Christ.' We do all this because we 'worship by the Spirit of God'. For this reason we 'put no confidence in the flesh'. In other words, we do not worship God because we are worthy to do so, nor do we rely on 'fleshly' feelings – worshipping only when human feelings are present. Rather, when we worship we are totally reliant on the Holy Spirit to prompt our minds and quicken our emotions to praise and glorify the Father and the Son.

FURTHER STUDY

Psa. 44:1–8; Gal. 6:14–18

1. What did the psalmist boast in God?
2. In what can we boast?

My Father and my God, I realise I am absolutely reliant on Your Spirit to worship You in the way You deserve. I give You all my willingness; now give me all Your power. In Jesus' name. Amen.

'Stop carping – start harping' TUES 22 OCT

FOR READING & MEDITATION – COLOSSIANS 1:1–14

'... joyfully giving thanks to the Father, who has qualified you to share in the inheritance of the saints ...' (vv.11–12)

No greater joy can fill the human heart than the joy that comes from knowing we have been transferred from the kingdom of darkness to the kingdom of God's beloved Son. Jesus' sacrifice sanctifies us and His Spirit empowers us to patiently endure everything that happens to us. Just look at what Paul has to say about giving thanks for this in his letter to the Colossians. Thanksgiving and praise punctuates almost every section of the letter.

We offer thanksgiving not grudgingly; rather, he talks about 'joyfully giving thanks to the Father'. Since we are established in Christ we can bear the fruit of praise, because we are building on the foundation of Jesus we can erect a house of worship, and as we are connected to the fountain of new life we can be 'overflowing with thankfulness' (2:7). Thus we need to 'stop carping and start harping', as C.H. Spurgeon once said.

Gratitude is like a river that flows through and refreshes every relationship (3:15). When we are grateful not only to God but are thankful, too, for each other then peace more than anything else will govern our lives and create harmony.

Thanksgiving transforms our prayers too (4:2). Nothing kills petition more swiftly than unthankfulness. Our prayers become just lists of complaints. Being thankful, even as we pray, strengthens our faith and lifts prayer out of self-absorption into the freedom of God. Thanksgiving helps to dissolve self-pity and enables us to 'be joyful always' (1 Thess. 5:16), not because we learn to play deceitful mental tricks on ourselves and praise God *for* everything but because, with the audacity of faith, we dare to praise God *in* everything (1 Thess. 5:18).

FURTHER STUDY

Phil. 4:4–7; 1 Thess. 5:16–28

1. How are we to pray?

2. What is God's will for us?

O Father, I am so challenged by the need to praise You in everything. Sometimes this is easier than at other times. Bring me to the point where I will praise You not in some things but in all things. In Jesus' name. Amen.

How we worship is crucial

FOR READING & MEDITATION – COLOSSIANS 3:1–17

'Let the word of Christ dwell in you richly as you teach and admonish one another ...' (v.16)

Christian worship is enriched by the Word of God and inspired by the Spirit of God. Both Word and Spirit are powerful ingredients for Christian worship. When Paul was writing to the Ephesians he emphasised the Spirit; when he was writing to the Colossians he emphasised the Word, as we see from our text for today.

Central to our worship as Christians is the message about Christ. Worship is, after all, our response to the gospel. As the good news is heard afresh we respond with joy and praise. Just as Israel celebrated the rescue from Egypt so we tell out the majesty of our Redeemer. We so often need to be reminded again and again that our songs and hymns are not to be merely echoes of our feelings but rather expressions of the truth of the gospel.

Paul insists also that Christian worship is essentially a corporate activity, hence the use both here and in Ephesians of the phrase 'one another'. We lose so much when we individualise everything. Of course, only individuals can grasp these exhortations, but what Paul has in view is the shared experience of worship when Christians come together. The content of our hymns and prayers matters because worshipping together is one way in which Paul says we 'teach and admonish one another'. In some sections of the Church there is a great need for the content of the songs sung in the services to be richer and more biblical so that the worship is deeper in tone and substance. How we worship is crucial because we affect each other profoundly. When the full message of who Jesus is informs our worship from start to finish then every worshipper's life is enriched in the process.

FURTHER STUDY

Psa. 119:161–168; Luke 2:25–38

1. How was the psalmist affected by God's Word?

2. How were Simeon and Anna affected by meeting Jesus?

O Gracious Father, again we cry: save us Your people from empty or superficial worship. We fail to understand so often in this regard. Help us see that the way we worship affects us either for good or bad. In Jesus' name. Amen.

An early Christian hymn

FOR READING & MEDITATION – 1 TIMOTHY 3:1–16

'... He appeared in a body, was vindicated by the Spirit, was seen by angels ...' (v.16)

The Christian understanding of worship, as we explored a few days ago, is distinctively Trinitarian – it is worship of the Father, Son and Holy Spirit. It was the experiences of the early apostles that gave rise to the doctrine of the Trinity. The apostles – all Jews to a man – already worshipped and prayed to the one Creator God. Then they met Jesus, and after His resurrection they came to see that He held the same status as God. At Pentecost the creative Spirit of God glorified Jesus to them so that, with heightened awareness, they came to worship both Jesus and God.

Martin Hengel, a leading German New Testament scholar, has observed that the high spots in the New Testament revelation of the divine status of Jesus occur in the passages that many scholars regard as early Christian hymns. Today's reading is one of them. We could have explored or highlighted other examples, such as Philippians 2:5–11 or Colossians 1:15–20. Hengel pondered how this amazing picture of Jesus as one with the eternal Creator God became known to the first believers. Perhaps, he suggested, it was while they were singing the psalms which speak of the coming of the ideal King, or Messiah, that the early Christian worshippers, filled with love for Jesus and with the Spirit, were inspired by the Holy Spirit to extend the boundaries of the psalms to embrace Jesus.

This sounds feasible, does it not? Didn't Jesus say that when the Holy Spirit came He would show His followers the truth about who He really is (John 16:13)? And when better to do this than when they were gathered together to worship? The Spirit does not give us a new revelation of Jesus, but He will give us a fresh vision of Him.

FURTHER STUDY

Psa. 45:1–9; Heb. 1:1–13

1. How might the Psalms relate to Jesus?

2. How did New Testament writers draw on the Old Testament?

Father, I see that although the revelation of Jesus is fixed, the Spirit is able to give us a continually fresh vision of Him. May I experience this in my life day by day. This I ask in Jesus' name. Amen.

The principal worshipper

FOR READING & MEDITATION – HEBREWS 2:1-13

'He says, "I will declare your name to my brothers; in the presence of the congregation I will sing your praises."' (v.12)

We find ourselves now in the book of Hebrews – a book in which the writer sometimes uses the Old Testament Scriptures in new and exciting ways to help us gain a deeper understanding of worship.

This is very evident from the text before us now. He takes the words of Psalm 22:22 and shows how they apply to the risen and ascended Jesus: '... in the presence of the congregation I will sing your praises'. What a wonderful and inspiring thought. This one insight alone, if we consider it carefully, can transform our whole attitude to worship.

This is what the writer is saying: whenever we gather for true spiritual worship, Jesus is the principal worshipper, leading us in praise! It was the famous nineteenth-century preacher, F.B. Meyer, who said, 'Whenever in the congregation of the saints there is an outburst of genuine song, you may detect the voice of Jesus singing with them and identifying with it.' How encouraging to know that when we come together to worship we are joining Jesus in His praise of the Father. But then, shouldn't everything we do as believers be done in the same way? Is not the bread that we break a means of sharing in the body of Christ? Is not the cup that we bless a means of sharing in the blood of Christ? Are not the songs that we sing a means of sharing in the praise Christ offers? Are not the prayers we pray a means of sharing in the high priestly intercession of Christ? Is not the Body we are building with love and spiritual gifts a means of sharing also in the very body of Christ? Is not the love we share a means of sharing in the mutual love of the Father and the Son?

FURTHER STUDY

John 12:28; 13:31–35

1. What did Jesus seek?

2. How can we share in the mutual love of the Father and Son?

Lord Jesus Christ, how exciting it is to know that when we are praising the Father You are the principal worshipper. Help me understand even more the full significance of this so that it may enrich the whole of my life. In Jesus' name. Amen.

The divine Intercessor

FOR READING & MEDITATION – HEBREWS 9:11–28

'For Christ ... entered heaven itself, now to appear for us in God's presence.' (v.24)

The letter to the Hebrews is exceptionally helpful when it comes to understanding what it means to worship God. One scholar, David Peterson, calls Hebrews 'the most complete and fully integrated theology of worship in the New Testament'. At the heart of this is the wonderful vision of Jesus, whose life was one long doxology of praise to the Father, and whose death was the full and final sacrifice for sins. This perfect life and complete sacrifice is portrayed in Hebrews as the only basis on which we can relate to God and come before Him to offer acceptable worship.

What is more, Hebrews is unique in the New Testament for giving us the picture of Jesus as our great High Priest. Jesus is alive at the Father's right hand and there He mediates for us. He makes His own self-offering perpetually available as the means of our acceptance and forgiveness. He takes our petitions and the offering of our lives and makes them acceptable to God. Above all, Jesus continues to make intercession for us as He pleads the merits of His blood on our behalf.

Pause and consider this: right now, as you read these notes, Jesus is praying for you! That thought must surely stir your heart to worship and praise. Jesus once said to Simon Peter, 'Satan has asked to sift you as wheat. But I have prayed for you, Simon, that your faith may not fail. And when you have turned back, strengthen your brothers' (Luke 22:31–32). How encouraging that must have been for Simon Peter. Doesn't the fact that Jesus is also praying for you, and knows the problems you may be facing, cause your soul to break forth in praise?

FURTHER STUDY

Heb. 7:22–28; 10:1–23

1. How often are you in Jesus' thoughts and prayers?

2. Contrast the blood of animals and the blood of Christ.

Lord Jesus Christ, it sounds almost too good to be true that You are interceding for me before Your Father's throne. But it is too good, also, not to be true. Receive at this moment my adoration and praise. Amen.

Everything to sing about

FOR READING & MEDITATION – JAMES 5:13–20

'Is anyone happy? Let him sing songs of praise.' (v.13)

James tells us that when we feel happy then we should sing. Gordon Fee said, 'Where the Spirit of God is there is also singing.' Throughout time the people of God have often broken out into song. The contemplation of God's goodness and power sometimes produces feelings so strong within us that they need to be expressed not just in spoken words but also in song. Our mouths were filled with laughter, our tongues with songs of joy' (Psa. 126:2) was the response of the Jewish people when their fortunes were restored. There are those who sing only when they are full of alcohol; there are people who sing because they just can't help singing.

Over the centuries many of God's servants have continued singing even in the most desperate situations. They are what we might call 'unsung heroes' – unsung but singing! Brother Yun, in *The Heavenly Man,* describes how, handcuffed and imprisoned for his faith, he was filled with joy as he used the handcuffs to bang on an old drum while he sang Psalm 150.

William Law wrote in his famous *Serious Call to a Devout and Holy Life* that singing clears the air for meeting God. 'There is nothing that so clears the way for your prayers,' he said, 'nothing that so disperses dullness of heart, nothing that so purifies the soul from poor and little passions, nothing that so opens heaven, or carries your heart so near to it, as ... songs of praise.' Whether we sing spontaneously because we are happy or choose to sing because we are in a difficult situation, singing carries our hearts nearer to God.

FURTHER STUDY

John 7: 37–39; Acts 16:22–34

1. Why can we not help singing God's praise?

2. Why can we praise God whatever our circumstances?

O God my Father, I realise that there are some who cannot sing because they have nothing to sing about. In You I have everything to sing about. I am so thankful. Amen.

'A theatre in the round'

MON
28 OCT

FOR READING & MEDITATION – REVELATION 5:1–14

'... "To him who sits on the throne and to the Lamb be praise and honour and glory and power, for ever and ever!"' (v.13)

In the book of Revelation (the book that puts everything in its true perspective) worship is seen as centred on the throne of God. Throughout the book it is God's sovereignty that is being celebrated. The message that comes through in Revelation is that there is a throne in the universe and that the One who sits on it has everything under control.

The theologian Barry Leisch says that worship in the book of Revelation is 'akin to a theatre in the round' because the book describes a series of concentric circles with the throne at the centre. Around the throne are four living creatures who represent the whole of creation and the twenty-four elders who represent the whole people of God viewed as priests (cf. 1 Chron. 24–25). Encircling them are myriads of angels so that the voice of every creature in heaven and earth is finally heard exulting God. The keynotes here are 'acclamation' as all heaven pays homage to the King, and 'adoration' as the elders prostrate themselves before the Sovereign Lord and cast their crowns at His feet (4:10).

Throne-centred worship reorientates our lives dramatically. As Eugene Peterson astutely puts it, 'In worship God gathers His people to Himself as the centre. Worship is a meeting at the centre so that our lives are centred on God and not lived eccentrically. We worship so that we live in response to and from the centre, the living God.' When our lives are reorientated around the throne we recover our poise and sense of purpose. How it helps to deepen our understanding of worship to know that at the centre of the universe there is an unassailable throne and that the One who sits on it is in full and complete control.

FURTHER STUDY

Psa. 89:1–16; Heb. 4:14–16

1. What is the nature of God's throne?

2. How does the nature of God's throne impact on our praise?

Great and Sovereign God, how reassuring it is to know that Your throne is unassailable and everlasting. I worship You, a God who is eternal. I am so grateful. Amen.

'The Church's magnificat'

FOR READING & MEDITATION – REVELATION 7:9–15

'And they cried out in a loud voice: "Salvation belongs to our God, who sits on the throne ..."' (v.10)

The sound of praise and worship echoes throughout the book of Revelation. Praise is given for the outworking of God's redemptive purposes and the certainty that God will reign for ever (11:15–18). There is praise for the fulfilment of all God's Old Testament promises which unite the believers of the Old Testament and the believers of the New Testament in one great song of praise – the song of Moses and the Lamb (15:3–4). Praise – with no ill-intent – is also given for God's final judgment on evil and human wickedness, to which the saints respond with glad 'Amens' and 'Hallelujahs' (19:1–8). Such praise is a universal song which extends out from the four living creatures (4:8) and 24 elders (4:10), through the 144,000 redeemed (7:4), that is, vast crowds too numerous to count (7:9), to include myriads of angels (5:11), until every living being is enlisted in the chorus (5:13).

And this outpouring of praise is a multi-media event! There is a rich variety of voices – those of the elders, angels, indeed, the whole creation; there are solo voices and vast cosmic choruses. Music is played on harps and lyres. Festal shouts, thunder and lightning, solemn silences, exuberant joy, colourful robes, rainbows, glittering jewels, and fragrant incense all have a part to play in the proceedings. It all constitutes what theologian G.C. Berkouwer called 'the magnificat of the Church triumphant'.

What is the reason for all this? It is prompted by the fact that God, in Christ, has made it possible for men and women to be cleansed from their sin and join Him in eternity. It's so simple, yet so sublime.

FURTHER STUDY

Luke 1:46–55; Rev. 19:1–9

1. For what reasons did Mary give her own magnificat?

2. For what reasons is praise given to God?

Father, there are so many reasons to praise You, but for me by far the greatest reason is the salvation You have procured for me through Your Son. For that I will never cease to praise You. Amen.

ORDER FORM

EDWJ S/O 2013

4 EASY WAYS TO ORDER:

1. Phone in your credit card order: **01252 784710** (Mon-Fri, 9.30am - 5pm)
2. Visit our Online Store at **www.cwr.org.uk/store**
3. Send this form together with your payment to:
   CWR, Waverley Abbey House, Waverley Lane, Farnham, Surrey GU9 8EP
4. Visit your local Christian bookshop

For a list of our National Distributors, who supply countries outside the UK, visit www.cwr.org.uk/distributors

YOUR DETAILS (REQUIRED FOR ORDERS AND DONATIONS)

Name:	**CWR ID No.** (if known):
Home Address:	
	Postcode:
Telephone No. (for queries):	**Email:**

PUBLICATIONS

TITLE	QTY	PRICE	TOTAL
Total publications			
All CWR adult Bible-reading notes are also available in ebook and email subscription format. Visit www.cwr.org.uk for further information.			
UK p&p: up to £24.99 = **£2.99**; £25.00 and over = **FREE**			
Elsewhere p&p: up to £10 = **£4.95**; £10.01 - £50 = **£6.95**; £50.01 - £99.99 = **£10**; £100 and over = **£30**			
Please allow 14 days for delivery — **Total publications and p&p A**			

SUBSCRIPTIONS* (NON DIRECT DEBIT)

SUBSCRIPTIONS	QTY	PRICE (INCLUDING P&P) UK	Europe	Elsewhere	TOTAL
Every Day with Jesus (1yr, 6 issues)		£15.95	£19.95	Please contact nearest National Distributor or CWR direct	
Large Print *Every Day with Jesus* (1yr, 6 issues)		£15.95	£19.95		
Inspiring Women Every Day (1yr, 6 issues)		£15.95	£19.95		
Life Every Day (Jeff Lucas) (1yr, 6 issues)		£15.95	£19.95		
Cover to Cover Every Day (1yr, 6 issues)		£15.95	£19.95		
Mettle: 14-18s (1yr, 3 issues)		£14.50	£16.60		
YP's: 11-15s (1yr, 6 issues)		£15.95	£19.95		
Topz: 7-11s (1yr, 6 issues)		£15.95	£19.95		
Total Subscriptions (Subscription prices already include postage and packing) **B**					

Please circle which bimonthly issue you would like your subscription to commence from:
Jan/Feb Mar/Apr May/Jun Jul/Aug Sep/Oct Nov/Dec

* Only use this section for subscriptions paid for by credit/debit card or cheque. For Direct Debit subscriptions see overleaf.

CONTINUED OVERLEAF >>

<< SEE PREVIOUS PAGE FOR START OF ORDER FORM

PAYMENT DETAILS

☐ I enclose a cheque/PO made payable to CWR for the amount of: **£** ______

☐ Please charge my credit/debit card.

Cardholder's name (in BLOCK CAPITALS) ______

Card No. ☐☐☐☐ ☐☐☐☐ ☐☐☐☐ ☐☐☐☐

Expires end ☐☐ ☐☐ Security Code ☐☐☐

GIFT TO CWR

☐ Please send me an acknowledgement of my gift **C**

GIFT AID (YOUR HOME ADDRESS REQUIRED, SEE OVERLEAF)

giftaid it

I am a UK taxpayer and want CWR to reclaim the tax on all my donations for the four years prior to this year **and on** all donations I make from the date of this Gift Aid declaration until further notice.*

Taxpayer's Full Name (in BLOCK CAPITALS) ______

Signature ______ **Date** ______

*I understand I must pay an amount of Income/Capital Gains Tax at least equal to the tax the charity reclaims in the tax year.

GRAND TOTAL (Total of A, B, & C)

SUBSCRIPTIONS BY DIRECT DEBIT (UK BANK ACCOUNT HOLDERS ONLY)

Subscriptions cost £15.95 (except *Mettle*: £14.50) for one year for delivery within the UK. Please tick relevant boxes and fill in the form bel

☐ *Every Day with Jesus* (1yr, 6 issues)
☐ Large Print *Every Day with Jesus* (1yr, 6 issues)
☐ *Inspiring Women Every Day* (1yr, 6 issues)
☐ *Life Every Day* (Jeff Lucas) (1yr, 6 issues)
☐ *Cover to Cover Every Day* (1yr, 6 issues)
☐ *Mettle*: 14-18s (1yr, 3 issues)
☐ *YP's*: 11-15s (1yr, 6 issues)
☐ *Topz*: 7-11s (1yr, 6 issues)

Issue to commence fro

☐ Jan/Feb ☐ Jul/Aug
☐ Mar/Apr ☐ Sep/Oct
☐ May/Jun ☐ Nov/Dec

CWR

Instruction to your Bank or Building Society to pay by Direct Debit

DIRECT Debit

Please fill in the form and send to: CWR, Waverley Abbey House, Waverley Lane, Farnham, Surrey GU9 8EP

Name and full postal address of your Bank or Building Society

To: The Manager Bank/Building Society

Address

Postcode

Name(s) of Account Holder(s)

Branch Sort Code

Bank/Building Society account number

Originator's Identification Number

4 2 0 4 8 7

Reference

Instruction to your Bank or Building Society

Please pay CWR Direct Debits from the account detailed in this Instruction subje to the safeguards assured by the Direct Debit Guarantee.
I understand that this Instruction may remain with CWR and, if so, details will be passed electronically to my Bank/Building Society.

Signature(s)

Date

Banks and Building Societies may not accept Direct Debit Instructions for some types of account